GW00372469

HMSO ✓
3.60

HOME OFFICE
ANIMALS (SCIENTIFIC PROCEDURES) ACT 1986

GUIDANCE ON THE OPERATION OF THE ANIMALS (SCIENTIFIC PROCEDURES) ACT 1986

Presented pursuant to Act Eliz. II 1986 C.14 Section 21
(Animals (Scientific Procedures) Act 1986)

Ordered by the House of Commons to be printed
14 February 1990

London: HMSO
£7.20 net

182

Contents

ANIMALS (SCIENTIFIC PROCEDURES) ACT 1986

GUIDANCE ON THE OPERATION OF THE ANIMALS (SCIENTIFIC PROCEDURES) ACT 1986

1 Introduction

1.1. The Animals (Scientific Procedures) Act 1986 regulates "any experimental or other scientific procedure applied to a protected animal which may have the effect of causing that animal pain, suffering, distress or lasting harm". The Act came into effect on 1 January 1987. A copy is at Appendix I.

1.2. This Guidance is issued under section 21 of the Act, following consultation with the Animal Procedures Committee under section 21(3), and applies throughout the United Kingdom. In Great Britain, the Act is administered by the Home Office. In Northern Ireland, it is administered by the Department of Health and Social Services on behalf of the Secretary of State for Northern Ireland. Where the Guidance speaks of "the Secretary of State" or "the Home Office" it means, in Northern Ireland, the Department of Health and Social Services.

1.3. The purpose of this Guidance is to explain the Act and:

(i) to set out how applications for licences and certificates are considered;

(ii) the terms and conditions under which licences and certificates are granted;

(iii) the arrangement for referral of applications to external assessors and/or the Animal Procedures Committee;

(iv) the responsibilities of certificate holders, licensees and named persons;

(v) how the Act is enforced;

(vi) the procedures for making representations under the Act.

1.4. From time to time, additional guidance may be issued on specific issues. Besides being published in the normal way, it may also be attached as an appendix to the Annual Report of the Animal Procedures Committee.

1.5. This Guidance is not intended to be exhaustive and, in cases of doubt, an Inspector appointed under section 18 of the Act should be consulted. The Inspectorate will always be prepared to discuss the preparation of applications for licences or certificates of designation.

Animals protected under the Act

1.6. A 'protected animal' is any living vertebrate, other than man. The Act therefore provides legal protection to all living vertebrates used in scientific procedures including certain immature forms which are protected from the following stages of development:

(i)   mammals, birds and reptiles: from halfway through gestation or incubation periods;

(ii)   fish and amphibians: from the time at which they become capable of independent feeding.

1.7.   Under section 1(3), the Home Secretary may by Order extend the definition of a protected animal and alter the stage of development at which the immature forms become protected.

1.8.   For the purposes of the Act, an animal is regarded as living until the permanent cessation of circulation or the destruction of the brain. Brain destruction is not complete in decerebrated animals: these are considered to be living and so protected under Act.

1.9.   In this Guidance, all references to "animals" should be taken as referring only to protected animals undergoing or expected to undergo scientific procedures or which are kept for the purpose of breeding animals for use in scientific procedures. Other legislation controls animals which are kept for purposes other than those regulated by the Act.

Regulated procedures

1.10.   Under section 2(1), a *regulated procedure* is any experimental or other scientific procedure which may have the effect of causing a protected animal pain, suffering, distress or lasting harm. These terms include death, disease, injury, physiological or psychological stress, significant discomfort or any disturbance to normal health, whether immediately or in the long term.

1.11.   A procedure is a regulated procedure if composed of a combination of non-regulated techniques which may have the effect described in paragraph 1.10.

1.12.   A procedure is also regulated if, following or during the course of a procedure performed for scientific purposes on an immature form, the animal reaches a stage of development (paragraph 1.6) at which it becomes a protected animal and the effect of that procedure is as described in paragraph 1.10.

1.13.   A procedure which may result in pain, suffering, distress or lasting harm to a fetus or immature form at or beyond the stage at which it becomes protected is regarded as a regulated procedure, irrespective of any effect on the parent animal. Anything which may result in the birth or hatching of a protected animal with abnormalities which may cause it pain, suffering, distress or lasting harm; for instance, the breeding of animals with harmful genetic defects, is a regulated procedure.

1.14.   These definitions remain true even if any pain, suffering, distress or lasting harm which would otherwise have resulted is mitigated or prevented by anaesthetics or other substances to sedate, restrain or dull perception, or by prior decerebration or other procedure for rendering the animal insentient.

1.15.   Under section 2(4) of the Act, the giving of an anaesthetic or analgesic or other substances to sedate, restrain or dull the perception of pain of a protected animal for scientific purposes is itself a regulated procedure (but see paragraphs 1.17 and 1.18). Likewise, decerebration, or any other procedure to render a protected animal insentient, if done for scientific purposes, is a regulated procedure.

Procedures which are not regulated

1.16.   Under section 2(5), the ringing, tagging or marking of an animal or any other humane procedure for the sole purpose of enabling an animal to be identified is not a regulated procedure if it causes only momentary pain or distress and no lasting harm. Methods of marking which may cause pain, suffering, distress or lasting harm, like toe clipping, are regulated when carried out for a scientific purpose.

1.17. A clinical test on animals for evaluating a veterinary product in accordance with section 32 of the Medicines Act 1968 or an Order under section 35(8)(b) of that Act is not a regulated procedure.

1.18. Procedures carried out for the purposes of recognised veterinary, agricultural or animal husbandry practice are not regulated under the Act. For example, taking blood or other tissue samples for diagnosis and giving established medicines by injection are recognised veterinary procedures, if done for the benefit of the animal, and so are exempt from the Act. Similarly, husbandry practices which may cause pain, like castration, are not regulated procedures unless they form part of a scientific study. Where there is doubt, the Inspector should be consulted.

Humane killing

1.19. The killing of a protected animal is a regulated procedure if the animal is killed for a scientific purpose in a designated establishment using a method which is not exempted by Schedule 1 to the Act. The Home Secretary has power to amend this Schedule by Order.

1.20. It follows that killing a protected animal in a designated establishment by a method listed in Schedule 1 is not a regulated procedure and does not require authorisation by a project or a personal licence. It is a condition of certificates of designation that such killing must be performed by a competent person.

1.21. Methods of humane killing other than those contained in Schedule 1 may be allowed provided that they are performed by competent personnel either as regulated procedures specified in the appropriate project and personal licences, or under authority conferred by a special condition in the certificate of designation.

Codes of Practice

1.22. Under section 21 of the Act, the Home Office has issued a *Code of Practice for the Housing and Care of Animals used in Scientific Procedures* (1989; HC 107). This is obtainable from HMSO. References in this Guidance to a Code of Practice should be taken as referring to this Code and any further Codes of Practice issued by the Home Office.

1.23. The Ministry of Agriculture, Fisheries and Food has issued, under section 3(1) of the Agriculture (Miscellaneous Provisions) Act 1968, MAFF Codes of Recommendations for the Welfare of Livestock which apply to farm animals, including domestic fowls.

Guidelines

1.24. The Universities' Federation for Animal Welfare has published voluntary guidelines for the recognition and assessment of pain, and the conduct of surgical procedures, and may issue further guidelines in this series. These are obtainable from UFAW at 8 Hamilton Close, South Mimms, Potters Bar, Herts EN6 3QD.

1.25. The Laboratory Animals Breeders Association has also issued Guidelines for the Care of Animals Bred for Scientific Purposes.

2 Designation of Scientific Procedure Establishments

2.1.   All places where regulated scientific procedures are performed must be designated under section 6 of the Act (but see paragraph 2.8).

2.2.   The certificate of designation will be issued to the person who represents the governing authority of the establishment and who is ultimately responsible to the Home Office for ensuring that the conditions of the certificate are observed.

2.3.   Under section 6(5), all applicants for certificates must nominate:

   (i)   one or more persons responsible for the day-to-day care of the animals;

   (ii)   one or more veterinary surgeons to provide advice on animal health and welfare.

2.4.   A person other than a veterinary surgeon may be accepted in respect of certain species when, after consultation with the Royal College of Veterinary Surgeons, it appears that no appropriate veterinary surgeon is available. In practice, this is unusual and has arisen mostly in relation to establishments in which work is confined to fish or to avian embryos.

2.5.   If the facilities provided are appropriate and those persons nominated for the care of the animals are suitably qualified, a certificate will be issued with certain standard and, where necessary, additional conditions. The standard conditions are at Appendix II.

Responsibilities of the certificate holder

2.6.   The responsibilities of the certificate holder include ensuring that:

   (i)   the Inspector is provided with reasonable access to all parts of the establishment listed on the certificate of designation;

   (ii)   named day-to-day care persons discharge their duties effectively;

   (iii)   the named veterinary surgeon(s) discharges his or her duties effectively and that the identity of any deputy is made known to the named day-to-day care person(s);

   (iv)   the fabric of the establishment is maintained in accordance with the *Code of Practice;*

   (v)   all scientific procedures on living animals conducted at the establishment are authorised by project and personal licences, that no unauthorised procedures take place and that a record is maintained of all project and personal licence holders;

   (vi)   the establishment is appropriately staffed at all times to ensure the well-being of all protected animals and that suitable arrangements are made to provide adequate care if the named persons are not available for any reason, such as leave or sickness;

   (vii)   there is always available a person competent to kill animals humanely using any Schedule 1 method appropriate to the species, or any other method listed in the certificate of designation and that any necessary equipment is readily available;

(viii) unless specifically authorised on a project licence, any *mouse, rat, guinea-pig, hamster, rabbit or primate* used, or held for use, in regulated procedures is obtained only from a designated breeder or supplier and that any *cat or dog* has been bred at and obtained from a designated breeding establishment;

(ix) all primates, dogs and cats are clearly marked by a method agreed with the Inspector;

(x) a protected animal is issued only to a suitably authorised person;

(xi) records are maintained of the source, use and final disposal of all animals protected by the Act in the establishment;

(xii) licensees, or applicants for licences, have reasonable access to facilities for education and training to meet their obligations under the Act;

(xiii) the Inspector is notified of any proposed change in the title of the establishment, the certificate holder, the name or qualifications of the named day-to-day care person(s) or named veterinary surgeon(s), the species of animal accommodated or the use of rooms listed in the certificate of designation.

Fees

2.7.   Under section 8, the holder of a certificate of designation is responsible for paying any fees under the Act. These are charged annually and currently consist of a flat rate annual fee and a fee for each personal licensee with primary availability (and therefore regarded as based) at the establishment at any time in the preceding calendar year. The fees and the basis on which they are charged may be varied from time to time in line with any changes in the cost of regulatory arrangements.

Regulated procedures at places other than designated establishments

2.8.   Under section 6 of the Act, it is possible for certain regulated procedures to be carried out in places which are not designated. This is normally done only when authority is required for a temporary period or when the procedures need to be performed in places which it is unrealistic or inappropriate to designate, such as rivers, woods or moorland. The authority to carry out procedures in places other than designated establishments will be specifically included in the project and personal licences, often with an additional special condition.

The named Day-to-Day Care Person

2.9.   Under section 6(5) of the Act, there must be at least one person named as having responsibility for the day-to-day care of the animals. This will often be a senior animal technician. In some establishments, it has been found to be convenient for several people to be named, with each taking responsibility for a discrete part of the establishment.

2.10.   Under section 6(6), the named day-to-day care person has to notify the personal licensee, or make arrangements for the care or destruction of the animal, if the health or welfare of any protected animal in the establishment gives rise to concern. In addition, his or her responsibilities include:

(i) being aware of the standards of husbandry and welfare set out in the *Code of Practice* and taking steps to ensure that these are met;

(ii) ensuring that suitable records are maintained of the health of the animals, in a form determined by the named veterinary surgeon with the agreement of the Inspector;

(iii) ensuring that suitable records are maintained of the environmental conditions in the rooms in which animals are held, and of all the animals bought, bred, supplied, issued, used, killed or otherwise disposed of;

(iv) knowing which areas of the establishment are listed in the certificate of designation and the purposes for which they are designated;

(v) ensuring that every protected animal in all designated areas is seen and checked at least once daily by a competent person;

(vi) being familiar with the project licences in use, including severity limits and severity conditions, adverse effects and humane endpoints;

(vii) knowing how to contact all project or personal licence holders, the named or deputy veterinary surgeon(s), and the certificate holder;

(viii) being aware of appropriate methods of killing listed in Schedule 1, together with any other approved methods listed in the certificate of designation and either being competent in their use or knowing how to contact someone who is.

The Named Veterinary Surgeon

2.11. Under section 6(6), if the health or welfare of any protected animal in the establishment gives rise to concern, the named veterinary surgeon has to notify the personal licensee, or make arrangements for the care or destruction of the animal. In addition, his or her responsibilities include:

(i) visiting all parts of the establishment designated in the certificate at a frequency which will allow the effective monitoring of the health status of the animals;

(ii) having regular contact with the certificate holder and the named day-to-day care person(s);

(iii) having a thorough knowledge of the prevention, diagnosis and treatment of disease which may affect the species kept, and of their husbandry and welfare requirements;

(iv) providing a comprehensive veterinary service at all times of the day or night throughout the year;

(v) supplying and directing the use of controlled drugs and other prescription-only medicines for use on protected animals in the establishment;

(vi) supervising the maintenance of health records relating to all protected animals in a form agreed with the Inspector: this should include a written record of advice or treatment given: these records should be kept at the establishment and be readily available to the named day-to-day care person, the certificate holder and the Inspector;

(vii) being familiar with the project licences in use, including severity limits and severity conditions, adverse effects and humane endpoints;

(viii) being able to advise licensees and others on appropriate methods of anaesthesia, analgesia and euthanasia, surgical technique, choice of species, and on the recognition of pain, suffering, distress or lasting harm;

(ix) being familiar with all methods of killing listed in Schedule 1 to the Act, together with any additional approved methods set out in the certificate of designation;

(x) certifying, where appropriate, that an animal is fit to travel to a specified place; to be used in further regulated procedures; to be released to the wild; or to be released for non-scientific purposes.

2.12.   The named veterinary surgeon should nominate deputies to provide cover for any absences and ensure that their identity is known to the certificate holder, the named day-to-day care person and other relevant staff in the establishment.

Named veterinary surgeons who hold project or personal licences

2.13.   Where the named veterinary surgeon also holds a project licence, a different veterinary surgeon should be nominated to perform the duties of the named veterinary surgeon for the project.

2.14.   Where the named veterinary surgeon holds only a personal licence, there is no need for a different person to be named as the veterinary surgeon for this work, unless there is a risk of a conflict of interest between the scientific outcome of the research and the welfare of the animals. If such a conflict of interest is thought likely to arise, it will be necessary to obtain the opinion of another veterinary surgeon (who should be identified on the certificate of designation) on matters relating to the health and welfare of the animals involved.

2.15.   Only in exceptional cases will these requirements be relaxed and this will require the prior agreement of the Inspector.

3 Designation of establishments for the breeding and supplying of animals for use in scientific procedures

3.1.   The Act contains specific safeguards to ensure that, whenever possible, animals which are used in scientific procedures have been specifically bred or obtained solely for that purpose. Schedule 2 to the Act lists the species of animals which can normally be obtained only from designated breeding or supplying establishments. Section 7 of the Act describes the procedures for designation of these establishments.

3.2.   The designation of breeding and supplying establishments is similar in principle to the designation of scientific procedure establishments. Many scientific procedure establishments also require additional designation as breeding or supplying establishments.

3.3.   A certificate of designation is granted only to those establishments which meet the required standards of animal husbandry and care. In broad terms, breeding and supplying establishments need to be able to provide facilities which are comparable with those in designated scientific procedure establishments. The standard conditions for breeding and supplying establishments are at Appendix III.

3.4.   Establishments which breed animals with harmful defects and those supplying surgically-prepared animals must be additionally designated as scientific procedure establishments. They need to accord, in all respects, with the requirements imposed on other scientific procedure establishments.

4 Project Licences

4.1. The project licence is the means by which authority is given for a programme of work involving regulated procedures on animals to be carried out in specified places by those who have appropriate personal licences (see paragraph 5.1). The project licence sets out the work which may be performed and the justification for the work. It is not concerned with the competence of licensees to carry out these procedures, since this is the purpose of the personal licence.

4.2. The scope of project licences can vary widely. A large project licence might cover, for example, the screening of drugs for medicinal use, involving a number of licensees using a range of animals. A smaller licence might cover the work of a single research student for a thesis, involving the investigation of one part of one system of one species and using few animals.

4.3. The application form for a project licence requires details of the proposed work to enable the justification for the application to be assessed. The details include:

    (i)   the purpose and scientific justification for the work;

    (ii)   a full description of the procedures which would be involved;

    (iii) an estimate of the number of animals of each species which may be required;

    (iv) a statement of the status, qualifications and experience of the project licence holder, so that an assessment can be made of the suitability of the applicant to supervise, manage and take responsibility for the project;

    (v)   an assessment of potential severity.

Assessment of benefit and severity

4.4. Section 5(4) of the Act requires that a project licence cannot be granted unless the likely adverse effects (pain, suffering, distress or lasting harm) of the procedures have been weighed against the benefit likely to accrue as a result of the proposed programme of work.

4.5. The benefit of work may sometimes be difficult to assess in advance and fundamental research where no immediate benefit is sought other than the increase of knowledge is valid and permissible. There is no intention of seeking to control or direct research by ascribing greater intrinsic merit to one area of research than to another so, in all cases, applicants should set out the potential benefit of their specific project, rather than, for instance, the importance of the topic in general.

4.6. Although it inevitably involves an element of subjectivity, applicants for project licences must assess the likely severity resulting from the procedures in order that this may be balanced against the potential benefit. It is, therefore, necessary to distinguish between assessment of the potential severity of individual procedures (or series of procedures) and the overall severity of the project. No work, however mild, will be permitted unless it can be justified. It is recognised that research into life-threatening disease may necessitate a degree of severity which might be difficult to justify in other research.

The severity of procedures

4.7.   In assessing the severity of a series of regulated procedures, account should be taken of the effect of all the procedures (whether regulated or not) applied to each animal or group of animals; the nature of any likely adverse effects; the action taken to mitigate these effects; and the endpoints applying to the procedures.

4.8.   Such an assessment should reflect the maximum severity expected to be experienced by any animal. It should not take into account the numbers of animals which might experience the maximum severity or the proportion of the animal's lifetime for which it might experience severe effects. Procedures throughout which the animal is either decerebrate or under general anaesthesia and is killed without recovering consciousness are regarded as unclassified.

Examples of severity of different procedures

4.9.   It is not possible to lay down hard and fast rules about how potential severity should be assessed. The taking of small or infrequent blood samples; skin irritation tests with substances expected to be only mildly irritant; conventional minor surgical procedures under anaesthesia such as laparoscopy, small superficial tissue biopsies or cannulation of peripheral blood vessels; are likely to be regarded as mild unless there is significant combination or repetition of procedures using the same animal. So will other procedures which will be terminated before the animal shows more than minor changes from normal behaviour.

4.10.   Many procedures are likely to be assessed as moderate. This could include much of the screening and development of potential pharmaceutical agents; toxicity tests avoiding lethal endpoints; and most surgical procedures, provided that suffering can be controlled by reliable post-operative analgesia and care.

4.11.   Procedures will be regarded as being of substantial severity if they result in a major departure from the animal's usual state of health or well-being. These are likely to include acute toxicity procedures where significant morbidity or death is an endpoint; some efficacy tests of antimicrobial agents and vaccines; some models of disease and major surgery where significant post-operative suffering may result. If it were expected that a single animal would suffer substantial effects, the procedure would warrant a severity limit of 'substantial'.

Humane endpoints

4.12.   Licence holders should always familiarise themselves with the signs of pain, discomfort and distress in the species they are using, by consultation with experienced colleagues, the person in charge of the day-to-day care of the animals and the named veterinary surgeon, and by reference to the guidelines mentioned in paragraph 1.24.

4.13.   It is often possible to reduce the severity of procedures by the use of appropriate endpoints and project licence applications involving procedures which may have specific adverse effects should, wherever possible, specify the particular action which the applicant intends to take in order to mitigate these effects. This will include, where appropriate, withdrawing the animal from the procedure, or humane killing.

The overall severity of a project

4.14.   The assessment of the overall severity of a project will reflect the cumulative effect of each procedure; the number of animals used in each procedure; the frequency of use of each procedure; the proportion of animals that are expected to be exposed to the upper limits of severity in each procedure; and the length of time that the animals might be exposed to the upper limits of severity.

4.15.   This assessment of overall severity will be used to weigh the likely adverse effects on all the animals against the benefits likely to accrue, as required by section 5(4) of the Act.

4.16.   The assessments of severity are not immutable and may be varied in the light of experience, for instance, when it transpires that an earlier endpoint would be equally acceptable scientifically, but would involve a lower level of suffering by the animal.

The severity condition

4.17.   Licence holders are required by conditions in both project and personal licences to minimise any pain, suffering or distress and they should approach the limit of severity which has been authorised only when absolutely necessary.

4.18.   All project licences contain a condition controlling the severity of procedures. This will reflect the severity limits which have been given to the procedures and the upper limit of severity which will be allowed on any one animal. The severity condition on the licence will be regarded as breached if the Inspector has not been notified when any protected animal has suffered significantly more as the result of a regulated procedure than has been authorised.

4.19.   It is not regarded as a breach of the condition if an animal has suffered more than authorised either unexpectedly or for extraneous reasons, for instance as the result of an intercurrent infection unrelated to the procedures. In all such cases, steps must be taken to alleviate the suffering at once.

4.20.   If it seems likely that the severity limit for a procedure may be exceeded, the project or personal licence holder will either terminate the procedure or advise the Inspector, who may, in certain circumstances, temporarily authorise a higher severity limit for a period of up to fourteen days. If necessary, an application should be made to amend the project licence.

Re-use of animals

4.21.   Section 14 of the Act sets out the conditions under which protected animals may be re-used. Section 14(1) takes precedence over section 14(2) as the statement of intent. Section 14(2) qualifies what would otherwise be a blanket ban on any re-use after a *series of regulated procedures for a particular purpose* which involved general anaesthesia and recovery of consciousness. Section 14(3) bans any re-use without permission after a *series of regulated procedures for a particular purpose* which did not involve general anaesthesia. **All** re-use must therefore be specifically authorised in advance.

4.22.   In general, if the same animal is being used as a matter of necessity, as in a *series of regulated procedures for a particular purpose*, this is not regarded as re-use. For example, where it is necessary to know how an animal responded to drugs A, B and C before interpreting its response to drug D, there is no choice and the successive use of the animal constitutes a single series of procedures without re-use.

4.23.   By contrast, if the procedures are unrelated or a different animal could equally well have been chosen for the second or subsequent procedures, use of the same animal is regarded as re-use. For example if, by choice, repeated samples of normal blood were taken from a rabbit, but each sample could equally well have come from a fresh rabbit, this would count as re-use and would require specific authority.

4.24. Where a protected animal has been subjected to a *series of regulated procedures for a particular purpose* (the first use), and as part of that is given a general anaesthetic, then the animal may not be used again in any regulated procedures for a different purpose. The only exceptions are:

(i) if the procedure, or each procedure, for which the anaesthetic was given consisted only of surgical preparation for a subsequent procedure; or

(ii) if the general anaesthetic was given solely to immobilise the animal, for instance, for the safety and/or comfort of the animal and/or the operator; or

(iii) if, during subsequent re-use, the animal is kept under general anaesthesia from which it is not allowed to recover consciousness.

4.25. Where a protected animal has been subjected to a *series of regulated procedures for a particular purpose* (the first use) but has **not** been given a general anaesthetic then, provided the first use is complete and the animal has fully recovered, it is possible for authority to be given for the animal to be used for further regulated procedures.

4.26. A *series of regulated procedures for a particular purpose* can normally be taken as corresponding to a single complete protocol (in section 19b of the project licence). It follows that any use of the animal on the same protocol again, or on another protocol, whether on the same licence or on another, will constitute re-use and so would require specific authority in the project licence (section 19b).

4.27. Section 14(2)(a) provides that surgically-prepared animals may (subject to permission) be re-used for subsequent procedures provided that the purpose remains the same and that the surgical preparation was essential for each of the subsequent uses. Thus, a dog which has been surgically prepared under general anaesthesia with a carotid loop to test cardiovascular drugs may (subject to permission) be successively used for several such drugs, provided that the tests all require the carotid loop.

4.28. Since project licences are theme based, it follows that, with rare exceptions, movement of an animal from one project to another would involve some change of purpose, however subtle. This will generally preclude the movement between projects of an animal which has been subjected to regulated procedures under general anaesthetic. Exceptions will be animals prepared under a project licence where the declared purpose is to prepare animals for use under another project licence and animals re-used under terminal anaesthesia.

4.29. Because of section 14(2)(b), an animal given a general anaesthetic solely to immobilise it may be re-used (subject to permission) in exactly the same way as an animal to which no anaesthetic has been administered. It is necessary to decide on a case by case basis as to whether the anaesthetic is given to prevent the animal feeling pain or to make the procedure easier for the operator or the animal by restraining or immobilising the animal. Implicit in the latter alternative is the assumption that the procedure is mild enough to be carried out without anaesthesia with a tractable, cooperative animal.

Referral of licence applications to an external assessor and to the Animal Procedures Committee

4.30. Under section 9(1), all applications for certificates and licences are assessed by one or more Inspectors. In certain cases, before a licence or certificate is granted, it may be referred to an external assessor, the Animal Procedures

Committee or to both. The Animal Procedures Committee considers all project licence applications involving cosmetics; tobacco or tobacco products (except where the animals are terminally anaesthetised); work of substantial severity on primates; and the acquisition or maintenance of manual skills for microsurgery.

4.31. The Committee will not usually consider other individual applications unless a general question about the permissibility of a certain type of procedure is at issue.

Other factors taken into account in considering project licence applications

4.32. Besides weighing the benefits of a project against the likely adverse effects on the animals concerned, a number of other considerations are taken into account before a project licence is granted. These include:

(i) the suitability of the design of the project in relation to its stated objectives;

(ii) the consideration which has been given by the applicant to reducing the number of animals used, refining procedures to minimise suffering and replacing animals with alternatives;

(iii) the justification for using the animals which are proposed, including the special justification required by section 5(6) for the use of primates, cats, dogs and equidae; and the sources from which Schedule 2 animals are to be obtained;

(iv) whether the proposed anaesthetic techniques or other methods for mitigating or preventing pain and distress are appropriate to the animals and procedures;

(v) whether the facilities at the establishment are adequate for the scientific procedures;

(vi) whether the place where the work is to be done has adequate facilities, in accordance with the *Code of Practice*, for the species involved.

4.33. Regulated procedures which are performed on contract for another organisation must normally be conducted under a project licence obtained by the organisation carrying out the work. In all cases, the project licence holder must be a person working in the United Kingdom.

4.34. All project licences will be governed by a set of conditions, some of which may be tailored to the specific requirements of the project. The standard conditions for project licences are set out in Appendix IV.

Responsibilities of the Project Licence Holder

4.35. Under section 5(2), the project licence holder is responsible for the direction, management and supervision of the project. This entails ensuring:

(i) that the project is conducted legally under the terms of the Act and in accordance with the conditions of the project licence;

(ii) that the programme of work keeps within the permitted purposes stated in the licence application;

(iii) that only the authorised species of animal and numbers of animals are used;

(iv) that personal licensees have authority for the regulated procedures which they carry out as part of the project;

(v) that all licensees are aware of and comply with the severity conditions of the project licence;

(vi) that personal licensees receive appropriate training, guidance and supervision to enable them to meet their responsibilities;

(vii) that full and accurate records are kept (see Appendix V);

(viii) that personal licensees ensure that all animals involved in the project are appropriately marked or identified.

4.36.   Although paragraph 3.4 of the *Code of Practice for the Housing and Care of Animals used in Scientific Procedures* makes it clear that the personal licensee bears primary responsibility for all animals submitted to procedures under the terms of his or her licence, the project licence holder is also listed as having responsibility for the care of these animals, particularly because he or she will often be in a more senior management position.

Statistical return of procedures

4.37.   The project licence holder is responsible also for making the statistical return of procedures for the project by 31 January each year, in accordance with the code lists and explanatory notes issued by the Home Office on how this should be done.

Deputy Project Licence Holder

4.38.   Only one person may hold a project licence so joint applications are not acceptable. Most project licences will require at least one deputy, particularly:

(i)   where the nature or scope of the project is such that control is best exercised through one or more deputy project licence holders;

(ii)   where work is to be done at more than one place so that a deputy is available locally to supervise the work on the project licence holder's behalf;

(iii)   where the project licence holder is likely to be absent for more than a month at a time;

(iv)   where the project licence holder does not hold a personal licence, in which case at least one deputy who holds a personal licence is required.

4.39.   The deputy project licence holder must be in a position to exercise day-to-day control over the work and to cover for the project licence holder's absence. His or her identity must be made known to those working on the project. A deputy project licence holder will normally hold, or have held, a personal licence.

Project licences for education and training

4.40.   Section 5(3)(e) provides that project licences may be issued for education and training. The severity limit of procedures in such projects will usually be "unclassified" or not more than moderate. In applying for a licence, applicants must show that they have carefully considered alternatives, such as video material and computer simulations, and that none is suitable.

4.41.   There are four principal types of procedures likely to be authorised by such a licence:

(i)   project licence authority may be issued for demonstrations of known facts or procedures which cannot be taught effectively by other means. These may be permitted in medical and veterinary schools, hospitals, colleges and in other scientific establishments, as part of training courses (for instance, in the practice of anaesthesia) and meetings of learned societies.

(ii) project licences may be granted to senior staff, such as departmental heads, for procedures for education of undergraduate or postgraduate students holding personal licences under their supervision.

(iii) at present, project licences for acquiring manual skills are granted only for regulated procedures on rats under terminal anaesthesia where the purpose is to teach microsurgery to those who will practice it clinically.

(iv) project licence authority may also be allowed for the performance of procedures for the purposes of making a film or recording for those educational or teaching purposes permitted under the Act. Permission is not required for the filming or recording of procedures in a project authorised for any other purpose, but section 16 of the Act forbids demonstrations to the general public, including live television.

4.42.   Under section 5(3)(e), project licences cannot be issued for education or training in primary or secondary schools.

5 Personal Licences

5.1.   Under section 3 of the Act, regulated procedures on living animals may not be performed on the authority of a project licence alone. There must be also a personal licence which is given only to those who are competent to perform the procedures, if necessary under supervision. Equally, a personal licence is not of itself authorisation to carry out any regulated procedure unless this has also been authorised by a project licence.

5.2.   All personal licences will be governed by conditions, some of which may be tailored to the personal licensee. The standard conditions which are applied to personal licences are listed at Appendix VI.

5.3.   Before carrying out any regulated procedure, it is the responsibility of personal licensees to ensure that the procedure is authorised by a project licence and is being carried out at a place specified in both the project and personal licences.

5.4.   Applicants for personal licences must be at least 18 years of age and:

(i)   be competent to take primary responsibility for the animals involved in procedures;

(ii)   have appropriate education and training;

(iii)   know the relevant techniques for the species concerned;

(iv)   know the signs of pain, suffering or distress in the species to be used;

(v)   understand the needs for any aftercare following the procedure;

(vi)   know how to care for the animals.

5.5.   It is normally expected that personal licensees should have at least the equivalent of five GCSEs at Grade C or above, or appropriate formal vocational training. A restricted licence may be issued to someone without these qualifications provided that it can be shown that the applicant has the necessary skill for the particular work. Most new licensees will be expected to work under supervision initially and, if so, conditions to this effect will be attached to the personal licence.

5.6.   Applicants who have not previously held a licence must provide a certificate signed by a sponsor that they fulfil the requirements in paragraph 5.4. The sponsor will normally be a senior member of staff in a position of authority at the applicant's place of work and will often be a project licence holder and hold, or have held, a personal licence.

5.7.   The sponsor must be in a position to know about the applicants' training, qualifications, experience and character and be able to give an opinion on their suitability to hold a licence and take responsibility for the care of the animals. Sponsors must list their own qualifications.

5.8.   In the case of applicants who do not have English as a native language, the sponsor must confirm the applicant's ability to understand English, the Act's provisions, the conditions of the project and personal licences, and the responsibilities of the personal licensee.

5.9.   Since a personal licence is a certificate of competence to perform regulated procedures on animals, personal licensees are not generally restricted to working on particular projects. However, new licensees will sometimes be confined to particular projects initially.

5.10.   Personal licences, like project licences, specify the place where the procedures may be carried out. Licensees who wish to extend or vary the availability of their licence to other places or perform additional procedures must apply formally for the licence to be amended.

Responsibility for the health and welfare of animals

5.11.   It is particularly important for personal licensees to appreciate that, as set out in paragraph 3.4 of the *Code of Practice for the Housing and Care of Animals used in Scientific Procedures*, they bear primary responsibility for the care of animals on which they have carried out scientific procedures.

5.12.   It is the responsibility of personal licensees to familiarise themselves with the severity limit of procedures listed in the project licence (section 19a) and the constraints upon adverse effects described in the protocol sheets (section 19b).

5.13.   Personal licensees should ensure that the cages, pens or places in which the animals are held carry labels indicating the project licence number, the personal licensee, the procedures which the animals are undergoing and any additional information which may be required by the Inspector.

Delegation of work to assistants

5.14.   Under section 10(4), personal licensees may delegate certain tasks to assistants, if the personal licence contains specific authority to do so. The circumstances in which certain regulated procedures may be delegated to assistants will vary. General examples of the kinds of procedures for which authority to delegate may be given are set out in Appendix VII.

6 Validity of certificates and licences and amendments to them

Certificates of designation

6.1.   Certificates of designation remain in force until suspended or revoked. The holder of a certificate of designation may apply at any time for a variation of the certificate, for instance when permission is required to keep different animals or to alter the rooms where they are kept. A change of certificate holder, for instance on retirement, will require the issue of a new certificate.

6.2.   Applications for permanent changes to the certificate of designation must always be submitted in writing with, where necessary, plans showing any proposed alterations to the premises. The Inspector has authority to grant temporary changes such as permission to hold animals in particular rooms overnight.

Project licences

6.3.   Section 5 of the Act permits a project licence to be valid for up to five years. Any fresh application to continue the programme of work should be made well in advance of the expiry date to allow good time for the application to be considered including, if necessary, referral to an external assessor or to the Animal Procedures Committee.

6.4.   A project licence terminates on the death of the licence holder but, under section 5(8), may continue in force temporarily if the Home Office is notified by the certificate holder or a representative within seven days of learning of the death of the project licence holder.

6.5.   Project licences cannot be transferred from one person to another and where it is necessary to change the project licence holder, on death or otherwise, a fresh application is necessary, although in some cases this may be in similar terms to the existing licence.

Personal licences

6.6.   Except when issued to students and others for the purpose of a course of study, personal licences generally remain in force indefinitely but are reviewed, under section 4(5), at least once every five years.

Amendments to certificates and licences

6.7.   Because of the detail in certificates and licences, it will often be necessary to amend them. An application form for this purpose will be provided whenever a certificate or licence is granted. Significant amendments, like the initial application, should be discussed in the first instance with the Inspector.

6.8.   Certificates of designation, project licences or personal licences may be varied on the authority of the Secretary of State at any time under section 11 of the Act and the procedure for making any representations against this under section 12 is set out in Appendix VIII and Appendix IX.

7 Infringements, Offences and Penalties

7.1.   Sections 22, 23 and 24 of the Act set out the offences created by the Act and the penalties for committing these offences.

7.2.   For most of the offences, the penalty on conviction on indictment is imprisonment for up to two years or a fine or both; or, on summary conviction, imprisonment for up to six months or a fine or both.

7.3.   The standard conditions on project and personal licences specify those actions which would be an offence under the Act and licence holders should familiarise themselves with these conditions.

Infringements

7.4.   Infringements vary from the technical to the very serious. In many cases, they can lead to a variation in the conditions of certificates or licences since, in addition to criminal proceedings, section 11 of the Act gives powers to vary or revoke licences where there has been a breach of a condition, or on other grounds. Variations in the conditions of a certificate or a licence will be specifically aimed at preventing a repetition of the infringement.

7.5.   This means that, regardless of whether an offence has been committed, infringement of the conditions of a licence is a serious matter. Subsequent infringements may well result in the licence being revoked and the work having to be discontinued.

7.6.   Following notification of a possible infringement, certificate holders and licensees will be informed whether the case is being referred to the Director of Public Prosecutions to be taken forward as criminal proceedings. In the case of licence holders, this notification will be copied additionally to the certificate holder in the establishment where the alleged infringement took place.

Variations imposed under section 12

7.7.   In those cases where it is not intended to prosecute, the certificate holder or licence holder will be notified as to whether the Secretary of State intends to revoke or vary the certificate or licence, or both.

7.8.   In some cases, particularly those which affect a project licence, it may be considered necessary for the project to be supervised in future by another project licence holder. Since licences cannot be transferred from one person to another, this will necessitate revoking the licence so that a fresh application can be made in the name of another project licence holder.

7.9.   Section 12 of the Act sets out the procedure for making representations against the revocation or variation of a licence or certificate. Under section 12(2) a notice revoking or varying a licence has to be accompanied by particulars of the rights to make representations. A copy of this notice is set out in Appendix VIII and the rules under which representations are made are set out in Appendix IX.

Appendix I:

Animals (Scientific Procedures) Act 1986

CHAPTER 14

ARRANGEMENT OF SECTIONS

Preliminary

Animals (Scientific Procedures) Act 1986

1986 CHAPTER 14

An Act to make new provision for the protection of
animals used for experimental or other scientific
purposes. [20th May 1986]

B E IT ENACTED by the Queen's most Excellent Majesty, by and
with the advice and consent of the Lords Spiritual and
Temporal, and Commons, in this present Parliament
assembled, and by the authority of the same, as follows:—

Preliminary

1.—(1) Subject to the provisions of this section, " a protected animal " for the purposes of this Act means any living
vertebrate other than man.

Protected animals.

(2) Any such vertebrate in its foetal, larval or embryonic form
is a protected animal only from the stage of its development
when—

> (*a*) in the case of a mammal, bird or reptile, half the ges-
> tation or incubation period for the relevant species
> has elapsed ; and

> (*b*) in any other case, it becomes capable of independent
> feeding.

(3) The Secretary of State may by order—

> (*a*) extend the definition of protected animal so as to in-
> clude invertebrates of any description ;

> (*b*) alter the stage of development specified in subsection
> (2) above ;

(*c*) make provision in lieu of subsection (2) above as respects any animal which becomes a protected animal by virtue of an order under paragraph (*a*) above.

(4) For the purposes of this section an animal shall be regarded as continuing to live until the permanent cessation of circulation or the destruction of its brain.

(5) In this section " vertebrate " means any animal of the Sub-phylum Vertebrata of the Phylum Chordata and " invertebrate " means any animal not of that Sub-phylum.

Regulated procedures.

2.—(1) Subject to the provisions of this section, " a regulated procedure " for the purposes of this Act means any experimental or other scientific procedure applied to a protected animal which may have the effect of causing that animal pain, suffering, distress or lasting harm.

(2) An experimental or other scientific procedure applied to an animal is also a regulated procedure if—

(*a*) it is part of a series or combination of such procedures (whether the same or different) applied to the same animal ; and

(*b*) the series or combination may have the effect mentioned in subsection (1) above ; and

(*c*) the animal is a protected animal throughout the series or combination or in the course of it attains the stage of its development when it becomes such an animal.

(3) Anything done for the purpose of, or liable to result in, the birth or hatching of a protected animal is also a regulated procedure if it may as respects that animal have the effect mentioned in subsection (1) above.

(4) In determining whether any procedure may have the effect mentioned in subsection (1) above the use of an anaesthetic or analgesic, decerebration and any other procedure for rendering an animal insentient shall be disregarded ; and the administration of an anaesthetic or analgesic to a protected animal, or decerebration or any other such procedure applied to such an animal, for the purposes of any experimental or other scientific procedure shall itself be a regulated procedure.

(5) The ringing, tagging or marking of an animal, or the application of any other humane procedure for the sole purpose of enabling an animal to be identified, is not a regulated procedure if it causes only momentary pain or distress and no lasting harm.

(6) The administration of any substance or article to an animal by way of a medicinal test on animals as defined in sub-section (6) of section 32 of the Medicines Act 1968 is not a regulated procedure if the substance or article is administered in

1968 c. 67.

accordance with the provisions of subsection (4) of that section or of an order under section 35(8)(*b*) of that Act.

(7) Killing a protected animal is a regulated procedure only if it is killed for experimental or other scientific use, the place where it is killed is a designated establishment and the method employed is not one appropriate to the animal under Schedule 1 to this Act.

(8) In this section references to a scientific procedure do not include references to any recognised veterinary, agricultural or animal husbandry practice.

(9) Schedule 1 to this Act may be amended by orders made by the Secretary of State.

Personal and project licences

3. No person shall apply a regulated procedure to an animal unless— Prohibition of unlicensed procedures.

  (*a*) he holds a personal licence qualifying him to apply a regulated procedure of that description to an animal of that description ;

  (*b*) the procedure is applied as part of a programme of work specified in a project licence authorising the application, as part of that programme, of a regulated procedure of that description to an animal of that description ; and

  (*c*) the place where the procedure is carried out is a place specified in the personal licence and the project licence.

4.—(1) A personal licence is a licence granted by the Secretary of State qualifying the holder to apply specified regulated procedures to animals of specified descriptions at a specified place or specified places. Personal licences.

(2) An application for a personal licence shall be made to the Secretary of State in such form and shall be supported by such information as he may reasonably require.

(3) Except where the Secretary of State dispenses with the requirements of this subsection any such application shall be endorsed by a person who—

  (*a*) is himself the holder of a personal licence or a licence treated as such a licence by virtue of Schedule 4 to this Act ; and

  (*b*) has knowledge of the biological or other relevant qualifications and of the training, experience and character of the applicant ;

and the person endorsing an application shall, if practicable, be a person occupying a position of authority at a place where the applicant is to be authorised by the licence to carry out the procedures specified in it.

(4) No personal licence shall be granted to a person under the age of eighteen.

(5) A personal licence shall continue in force until revoked but the Secretary of State shall review each personal licence granted by him at intervals not exceeding five years and may for that purpose require the holder to furnish him with such information as he may reasonably require.

Project licences.

5.—(1) A project licence is a licence granted by the Secretary of State specifying a programme of work and authorising the application, as part of that programme, of specified regulated procedures to animals of specified descriptions at a specified place or specified places.

(2) A project licence shall not be granted except to a person who undertakes overall responsibility for the programme to be specified in the licence.

(3) A project licence shall not be granted for any programme unless the Secretary of State is satisfied that it is undertaken for one or more of the following purposes—

  (a) the prevention (whether by the testing of any product or otherwise) or the diagnosis or treatment of disease, ill-health or abnormality, or their effects, in man, animals or plants;

  (b) the assessment, detection, regulation or modification of physiological conditions in man, animals or plants;

  (c) the protection of the natural environment in the interests of the health or welfare of man or animals;

  (d) the advancement of knowledge in biological or behavioural sciences;

  (e) education or training otherwise than in primary or secondary schools;

  (f) forensic enquiries;

  (g) the breeding of animals for experimental or other scientific use.

(4) In determining whether and on what terms to grant a project licence the Secretary of State shall weigh the likely adverse effects on the animals concerned against the benefit likely to accrue as a result of the programme to be specified in the licence.

(5) The Secretary of State shall not grant a project licence unless he is satisfied that the applicant has given adequate consideration to the feasibility of achieving the purpose of the programme to be specified in the licence by means not involving the use of protected animals.

(6) The Secretary of State shall not grant a project licence authorising the use of cats, dogs, primates or equidae unless he is satisfied that animals of no other species are suitable for the purposes of the programme to be specified in the licence or that it is not practicable to obtain animals of any other species that are suitable for those purposes.

(7) Unless revoked and subject to subsection (8) below, a project licence shall continue in force for such period as is specified in the licence and may be renewed for further periods but (without prejudice to the grant of a new licence in respect of the programme in question) no such licence shall be in force for more than five years in all.

(8) A project licence shall terminate on the death of the holder but if—

    (*a*) the holder of a certificate under section 6 below in respect of a place specified in the licence; or

    (*b*) where by virtue of subsection (2) of that section the licence does not specify a place in respect of which there is such a certificate, the holder of a personal licence engaged on the programme in question,

notifies the Secretary of State of the holder's death within seven days of its coming to his knowledge the licence shall, unless the Secretary of State otherwise directs, continue in force until the end of the period of twenty-eight days beginning with the date of the notification.

Designated establishments

6.—(1) Subject to subsection (2) below, no place shall be specified in a project licence unless it is a place designated by a certificate issued by the Secretary of State under this section as a scientific procedure establishment.

Scientific procedure establishments.

(2) Subsection (1) above shall not apply in any case in which it appears to the Secretary of State that the programme or procedures authorised by the licence require him to specify a different place.

(3) An application for a certificate in respect of a scientific procedure establishment shall be made to the Secretary of State in such form and shall be supported by such information as he may reasonably require.

(4) A certificate shall not be issued under this section—

    (*a*) except to a person occupying a position of authority at the establishment in question ; and

    (*b*) unless the application nominates for inclusion in the certificate pursuant to subsection (5) below a person or persons appearing to the Secretary of State to be suitable for that purpose.

(5) A certificate under this section shall specify—

    (*a*) a person to be responsible for the day-to-day care of the protected animals kept for experimental or other scientific purposes at the establishment ; and

    (*b*) a veterinary surgeon or other suitably qualified person to provide advice on their health and welfare ;

and the same person may, if the Secretary of State thinks fit, be specified under both paragraphs of this subsection.

(6) If it appears to any person specified in a certificate pursuant to subsection (5) above that the health or welfare of any such animal as is mentioned in that subsection gives rise to concern he shall—

    (*a*) notify the person holding a personal licence who is in charge of the animal ; or

    (*b*) if there is no such person or it is not practicable to notify him, take steps to ensure that the animal is cared for and, if it is necessary for it to be killed, that it is killed by a method which is appropriate under Schedule 1 to this Act or approved by the Secretary of State.

(7) In any case to which subsection (6) above applies the person specified in the certificate pursuant to paragraph (*a*) of subsection (5) above may also notify the person (if different) specified pursuant to paragraph (*b*) of that subsection ; and the person specified pursuant to either paragraph of that subsection may also notify one of the inspectors appointed under this Act.

(8) A certificate under this section shall continue in force until revoked.

Breeding and supplying establishments.

7.—(1) A person shall not at any place breed for use in regulated procedures (whether there or elsewhere) protected animals of a description specified in Schedule 2 to this Act unless that place is designated by a certificate issued by the Secretary of State under this section as a breeding establishment.

(2) A person shall not at any place keep any such protected animals which have not been bred there but are to be supplied for use elsewhere in regulated procedures unless that place is designated by a certificate issued by the Secretary of State under this section as a supplying establishment.

(3) An application for a certificate in respect of a breeding or supplying establishment shall be made to the Secretary of State in such form and shall be supported by such information as he may reasonably require.

(4) A certificate shall not be issued under this section unless the application nominates for inclusion in the certificate pursuant to subsection (5) below a person or persons appearing to the Secretary of State to be suitable for that purpose.

(5) A certificate under this section shall specify—

    (*a*) a person to be responsible for the day-to-day care of the animals bred or kept for breeding at the establishment or, as the case may be, kept there for the purpose of being supplied for use in regulated procedures; and

    (*b*) a veterinary surgeon or other suitably qualified person to provide advice on their health and welfare;

and the same person may, if the Secretary of State thinks fit, be specified under both paragraphs of this subsection.

(6) If it appears to any person specified in a certificate pursuant to subsection (5) above that the health or welfare of any such animal as is mentioned in that subsection gives rise to concern he shall take steps to ensure that it is cared for and, if it is necessary for it to be killed, that it is killed by a method appropriate under Schedule 1 to this Act or approved by the Secretary of State.

(7) In any case to which subsection (6) above applies the person specified in the certificate pursuant to paragraph (*a*) of subsection (5) above may also notify the person (if different) specified pursuant to paragraph (*b*) of that subsection; and the person specified pursuant to either paragraph of that subsection may also notify one of the inspectors appointed under this Act.

(8) A certificate under this section shall continue in force until revoked.

(9) Schedule 2 to this Act may be amended by orders made by the Secretary of State.

8. The holder of a certificate issued under section 6 or 7 above shall pay such periodical fees to the Secretary of State as may be prescribed by or determined in accordance with an order made by him.

Fees.

Licences and designation certificates: general provisions

9.—(1) Before granting a licence or issuing a certificate under this Act the Secretary of State shall consult one of the inspectors appointed under this Act and may also consult an independent assessor or the Animal Procedures Committee established by this Act.

Consultation.

(2) Where the Secretary of State proposes to consult an independent assessor he shall notify the applicant of that fact, and in selecting the assessor he shall have regard to any representations made by the applicant.

Conditions.

10.—(1) Subject to the provisions of this section, a licence or certificate under this Act may contain such conditions as the Secretary of State thinks fit.

(2) The conditions of a personal licence shall include—

(*a*) a condition to the effect that the holder shall take precautions to prevent or reduce to the minimum consistent with the purposes of the authorised procedures any pain, distress or discomfort to the animals to which those procedures may be applied; and

(*b*) an inviolable termination condition, that is to say, a condition specifying circumstances in which a protected animal which is being or has been subjected to a regulated procedure must in every case be immediately killed by a method appropriate to the animal under Schedule 1 to this Act or by such other method as may be authorised by the licence.

(3) The conditions of a project licence shall, unless the Secretary of State considers that an exception is justified, include a condition to the effect—

(*a*) that no cat or dog shall be used under the licence unless it has been bred at and obtained from a designated breeding establishment; and

(*b*) that no other protected animal of a description specified in Schedule 2 to this Act shall be used under the licence unless it has been bred at a designated breeding establishment or obtained from a designated supplying establishment;

but no exception shall be made from the condition required by paragraph (*a*) above unless the Secretary of State is satisfied that no animal suitable for the purpose of the programme specified in the licence can be obtained in accordance with that condition.

(4) If the conditions of a personal licence permit the holder to use assistants to perform, under his direction, tasks not requiring technical knowledge nothing done by an assistant in accordance with such a condition shall constitute a contravention of section 3 above.

(5) The conditions of a certificate issued under section 6 above shall include a condition prohibiting the killing otherwise than by a method which is appropriate under Schedule 1 to this Act or approved by the Secretary of State of any protected animal kept at the establishment for experimental or other scientific

purposes but not subjected to a regulated procedure or required to be killed by virtue of section 15 below; and the conditions of a certificate issued under section 7 above shall include a condition prohibiting the killing otherwise than by such a method of an animal of a description specified in Schedule 2 to this Act which is bred or kept for breeding or, as the case may be, kept at the establishment for the purposes of being supplied for use in regulated procedures but not used, or supplied for use, for that purpose.

(6) The conditions of a certificate issued under section 6 or 7 above shall include conditions requiring the holder of the certificate—

(a) to secure that a person competent to kill animals in the manner specified by conditions imposed in accordance with subsection (5) above will be available to do so; and

(b) to keep records as respects the source and disposal of and otherwise relating to the animals kept at the establishment for experimental or other scientific purposes or, as the case may be, bred or kept for breeding there or kept there for the purposes of being supplied for use in regulated procedures.

(7) Breach of a condition in a licence or certificate shall not invalidate the licence or certificate but shall be a ground for its variation or revocation.

11. A licence or certificate under this Act may be varied or revoked by the Secretary of State— *Variation and revocation.*

(a) on the ground mentioned in section 10(7) above;

(b) in any other case in which it appears to the Secretary of State appropriate to do so; or

(c) at the request of the holder.

12.—(1) Where the Secretary of State proposes— *Right to make representations.*

(a) to refuse a licence or certificate under this Act; or

(b) to vary or revoke such a licence or certificate otherwise than at the request of the holder,

he shall serve on the applicant or the holder a notice of his intention to do so.

(2) The notice shall state the reasons for which the Secretary of State proposes to act and give particulars of the rights conferred by subsection (3) below.

(3) A person on whom a notice is served under subsection (1) above may make written representations and, if desired, oral representations to a person appointed for that purpose by the

Secretary of State if before such date as is specified in the notice (not being less than twenty-eight days after the date of service) he notifies the Secretary of State of his wish to do so.

(4) The holder of a licence or certificate who is dissatisfied with any condition contained in it may, if he notifies the Secretary of State of his wish to do so, make written representations and, if desired, oral representations to a person appointed for that purpose by the Secretary of State; but the making of such representations shall not affect the operation of any condition unless and until it is varied under section 11 above.

(5) The person appointed to receive any representations under this section shall be a person who holds or has held judicial office in the United Kingdom or a barrister, solicitor or advocate of at least seven years' standing and the Secretary of State may, if he thinks fit, appoint a person with scientific or other appropriate qualifications to assist the person receiving the representations in his consideration of them.

(6) The person appointed to receive any such representations shall after considering them make a report to the Secretary of State; and the Secretary of State shall furnish a copy of the report to the person who made the representations and take it into account in deciding whether to refuse the application or to vary or revoke the licence or certificate, as the case may be.

(7) The Secretary of State may by order make rules with respect to the procedure to be followed in the making and consideration of representations under this section, including provision requiring any such representations to be made within a specified time.

(8) A notice under subsection (1) above may be served either personally or by post.

Suspension in cases of urgency.

13.—(1) If it appears to the Secretary of State to be urgently necessary for the welfare of any protected animals that a licence or certificate under this Act should cease to have effect forthwith he shall by notice served on the holder suspend its operation for a period not exceeding three months.

(2) If during that period a notice of proposed variation or revocation of the licence or certificate is served under section 12 above but at the end of that period—

(a) the time for notifying the Secretary of State under subsection (3) of that section has not expired; or

(b) representations are to be or are being made in accordance with that subsection; or

(c) such representations have been made but the Secretary of State has not received or has not completed his

consideration of the report of the person to whom the
representations were made,

he may by notice served on the holder further suspend the licence
or certificate until he is able to decide whether to vary or revoke
it but no further suspension shall be for longer than three months
at a time.

(3) A notice under this section may be served personally or by
post.

Additional controls

14.—(1) Where a protected animal— Re-use of
protected
(a) has been subjected to a series of regulated procedures animals.
for a particular purpose ; and

(b) has been given a general anaesthetic for any of those
procedures and allowed to recover consciousness,

it shall not be used for any further regulated procedures.

(2) Subsection (1) above shall not preclude the use of an
animal with the consent of the Secretary of State if—

(a) the procedure, or each procedure, for which the anaesthetic was given consisted only of surgical preparation
essential for a subsequent procedure ; or

(b) the anaesthetic was administered solely to immobilise
the animal ; or

(c) the animal is under general anaesthesia throughout the
further procedures and not allowed to recover consciousness.

(3) Where a protected animal—

(a) has been subjected to a series of regulated procedures
for a particular purpose ; but

(b) has not been given a general anaesthetic for any of
those procedures,

it shall not be used for any further regulated procedures except
with the consent of the Secretary of State.

(4) Any consent for the purposes of this section may relate to
a specified animal or to animals used in specified procedures or
specified circumstances.

15.—(1) Where a protected animal— Killing
animals at
(a) has been subjected to a series of regulated procedures conclusion of
for a particular purpose ; and regulated
procedures.
(b) at the conclusion of the series is suffering or likely to
suffer adverse effects,

the person who applied those procedures, or the last of them, shall cause the animal to be immediately killed by a method appropriate to the animal under Schedule 1 to this Act or by such other method as may be authorised by the personal licence of the person by whom the animal is killed.

(2) Subsection (1) above is without prejudice to any condition of a project licence requiring an animal to be killed at the conclusion of a regulated procedure in circumstances other than those mentioned in that subsection.

Prohibition of public displays. **16.**—(1) No person shall carry out any regulated procedure as an exhibition to the general public or carry out any such procedure which is shown live on television for general reception.

(2) No person shall publish a notice or advertisement announcing the carrying out of any regulated procedure in a manner that would contravene subsection (1) above.

Neuro-
muscular
blocking
agents.
17. No person shall in the course of a regulated procedure—

(a) use any neuromuscular blocking agent unless expressly authorised to do so by the personal and project licences under which the procedure is carried out ; or

(b) use any such agent instead of an anaesthetic.

The inspectorate and the committee

Inspectors. **18.**—(1) The Secretary of State shall, with the consent of the Treasury as to numbers and remuneration, appoint as inspectors for the purposes of this Act persons having such medical or veterinary qualifications as he thinks requisite.

(2) It shall be the duty of an inspector—

(a) to advise the Secretary of State on applications for personal and project licences, on requests for their variation or revocation and on their periodical review ;

(b) to advise him on applications for certificates under this Act and on requests for their variation or revocation ;

(c) to visit places where regulated procedures are carried out for the purpose of determining whether those procedures are authorised by the requisite licences and whether the conditions of those licences are being complied with ;

(d) to visit designated establishments for the purpose of determining whether the conditions of the certificates in respect of those establishments are being complied with ;

(e) to report to the Secretary of State any case in which any provision of this Act or any condition of a licence or certificate under this Act has not been or is not being complied with and to advise him on the action to be taken in any such case.

(3) If an inspector considers that a protected animal is undergoing excessive suffering he may require it to be immediately killed by a method appropriate to the animal under Schedule 1 to this Act or by such other method as may be authorised by any personal licence held by the person to whom the requirement is addressed.

19.—(1) There shall be a committee to be known as the Animal Procedures Committee.

(2) The Committee shall consist of a chairman and at least twelve other members appointed by the Secretary of State.

(3) Of the members other than the chairman—

  (*a*) at least two-thirds shall be persons having such a qualification as is mentioned in subsection (4) below ; and

  (*b*) at least one shall be a barrister, solicitor or advocate,

but so that at least half of those members are persons who neither hold nor within the previous six years have held any licence under this Act or under the Cruelty to Animals Act 1876 ; and in making appointments to the Committee the Secretary of State shall have regard to the desirability of ensuring that the interests of animal welfare are adequately represented.

(4) The qualifications referred to in subsection (3)(*a*) above are full registration as a medical practitioner, registration as a veterinary surgeon or qualifications or experience in a biological subject approved by the Secretary of State as relevant to the work of the Committee.

(5) Members of the Committee shall be appointed for such periods as the Secretary of State may determine but no such period shall exceed four years and no person shall be reappointed more than once.

(6) Any member may resign by notice in writing to the Secretary of State ; and the chairman may by such a notice resign his office as such.

(7) The Secretary of State may terminate the appointment of a member if he is satisfied that—

  (*a*) for a period of six months beginning not more than nine months previously he has, without the consent of the other members, failed to attend the meetings of the Committee ;

  (*b*) he is an undischarged bankrupt or has made an arrangement with his creditors ;

The Animal
Procedures
Committee.

1876 c. 77.

(c) he is by reason of physical or mental illness, or for any other reason, incapable of carrying out his duties; or

(d) he has been convicted of such a criminal offence, or his conduct has been such, that it is not in the Secretary of State's opinion fitting that he should remain a member.

(8) The Secretary of State may make payments to the chairman by way of remuneration and make payments to him and the other members in respect of expenses incurred by them in the performance of their duties.

(9) The Secretary of State may also defray any other expenses of the Committee.

Functions of the Committee.

20.—(1) It shall be the duty of the Animal Procedures Committee to advise the Secretary of State on such matters concerned with this Act and his functions under it as the Committee may determine or as may be referred to the Committee by the Secretary of State.

(2) In its consideration of any matter the Committee shall have regard both to the legitimate requirements of science and industry and to the protection of animals against avoidable suffering and unnecessary use in scientific procedures.

(3) The Committee may perform any of its functions by means of sub-committees and may co-opt as members of any sub-committee any persons considered by the Committee to be able to assist that sub-committee in its work.

(4) The Committee may promote research relevant to its functions and may obtain advice or assistance from other persons with knowledge or experience appearing to the Committee to be relevant to those functions.

(5) The Committee shall in each year make a report on its activities to the Secretary of State who shall lay copies of the report before Parliament.

Miscellaneous and supplementary

Guidance, codes of practice and statistics.

21.—(1) The Secretary of State shall publish information to serve as guidance with respect to the manner in which he proposes to exercise his power to grant licences and certificates under this Act and with respect to the conditions which he proposes to include in such licences and certificates.

(2) The Secretary of State shall issue codes of practice as to the care of protected animals and their use for regulated procedures and may approve such codes issued by other persons.

(3) The Secretary of State shall consult the Animal Procedures Committee before publishing or altering any information

under subsection (1) above or issuing, approving, altering or approving any alteration in any code issued or approved under subsection (2) above.

(4) A failure on the part of any person to comply with any provision of a code issued or approved under subsection (2) above shall not of itself render that person liable to criminal or civil proceedings but—

 (*a*) any such code shall be admissible in evidence in any such proceedings ; and

 (*b*) if any of its provisions appears to the court conducting the proceedings to be relevant to any question arising in the proceedings it shall be taken into account in determining that question.

(5) The Secretary of State shall lay before Parliament—

 (*a*) copies of any information published or code issued by him under subsection (1) or (2) above and of any alteration made by him in any such information or code ; and

 (*b*) copies of any code approved by him under subsection (2) above and of any alteration approved by him in any such code ;

and if either House of Parliament passes a resolution requiring the information, code or alteration mentioned in paragraph (*a*) above, or the approval mentioned in paragraph (*b*) above, to be withdrawn the Secretary of State shall withdraw it accordingly ; and where he withdraws information published or a code issued by him or his approval of a code he shall publish information or issue or approve a code, as the case may be, in substitution for the information or code previously published, issued or approved.

(6) No resolution shall be passed by either House under subsection (5) above in respect of any information, code or alteration after the end of the period of forty days beginning with the day on which a copy of the information, code or alteration was laid before that House ; but for the purposes of this subsection no account shall be taken of any time during which Parliament is dissolved or prorogued or during which both Houses are adjourned for more than four days.

(7) The Secretary of State shall in each year publish and lay before Parliament such information as he considers appropriate with respect to the use of protected animals in the previous year for experimental or other scientific purposes.

Penalties for contraventions.

22.—(1) Any person who contravenes section 3 above shall be guilty of an offence and liable—

    (*a*) on conviction on indictment, to imprisonment for a term not exceeding two years or to a fine or to both;

    (*b*) on summary conviction, to imprisonment for a term not exceeding six months or to a fine not exceeding the statutory maximum or to both.

(2) Any person who, being the holder of a project licence—

    (*a*) procures or knowingly permits a person under his control to carry out a regulated procedure otherwise than as part of the programme specified in the licence; or

    (*b*) procures or knowingly permits a person under his control to carry out a regulated procedure otherwise than in accordance with that person's personal licence,

shall be guilty of an offence and liable to the penalties specified in subsection (1) above.

(3) Any person who—

    (*a*) contravenes section 7(1) or (2), 14, 15, 16 or 17 above; or

    (*b*) fails to comply with a requirement imposed on him under section 18(3) above,

shall be guilty of an offence and liable on summary conviction to imprisonment for a term not exceeding three months or to a fine not exceeding the fourth level on the standard scale or to both.

(4) A person shall not be guilty of an offence under section 3 or 17(*a*) above by reason only that he acted without the authority of a project licence if he shows that he reasonably believed, after making due enquiry, that he had such authority.

1911 c. 27.
1912 c. 14.

(5) A person guilty of an offence under section 1 of the Protection of Animals Act 1911 or section 1 of the Protection of Animals (Scotland) Act 1912 in respect of an animal at a designated establishment shall be liable to the penalties specified in subsection (1) above.

False statements.

23.—(1) A person is guilty of an offence if for the purpose of obtaining or assisting another person to obtain a licence or certificate under this Act he furnishes information which he knows to be false or misleading in a material particular or recklessly furnishes information which is false or misleading in a material particular.

(2) A person guilty of an offence under this section shall be liable on summary conviction to imprisonment for a term not exceeding three months or to a fine not exceeding the fourth level on the standard scale or to both.

24.—(1) A person is guilty of an offence if otherwise than for the purpose of discharging his functions under this Act he discloses any information which has been obtained by him in the exercise of those functions and which he knows or has reasonable grounds for believing to have been given in confidence.

(2) A person guilty of an offence under this section shall be liable—

    (*a*) on conviction on indictment, to imprisonment for a term not exceeding two years or to a fine or to both ;

    (*b*) on summary conviction, to imprisonment for a term not exceeding six months or to a fine not exceeding the statutory maximum or to both.

25.—(1) If a justice of the peace or in Scotland a sheriff is satisfied by information on oath that there are reasonable grounds for believing that an offence under this Act has been or is being committed at any place, he may issue a warrant authorising a constable to enter that place if need be by such force as is reasonably necessary, to search it and to require any person found there to give his name and address.

(2) A warrant under this section may authorise a constable to be accompanied by an inspector appointed under this Act and shall require him to be accompanied by such an inspector if the place in question is a designated establishment.

(3) Any person who—

    (*a*) intentionally obstructs a constable or inspector in the exercise of his powers under this section ; or

    (*b*) refuses on demand to give his name and address or gives a false name or address,

shall be guilty of an offence and liable on summary conviction to imprisonment for a term not exceeding three months or to a fine not exceeding the fourth level on the standard scale or to both.

26.—(1) No proceedings for—

    (*a*) an offence under this Act ; or

    (*b*) an offence under section 1 of the Protection of Animals Act 1911 which is alleged to have been committed in respect of an animal at a designated establishment,

shall be brought in England and Wales except by or with the consent of the Director of Public Prosecutions.

(2) Summary proceedings for an offence under this Act may (without prejudice to any jurisdiction exercisable apart from this subsection) be taken against any person at any place at which he is for the time being.

1980 c. 43. (3) Notwithstanding anything in section 127(1) of the Magistrates' Courts Act 1980, an information relating to an offence under this Act which is triable by a magistrates' court in England and Wales may be so tried if it is laid at any time within three years after the commission of the offence and within six months after the date on which evidence sufficient in the opinion of the Director of Public Prosecutions to justify the proceedings comes to his knowledge.

1975 c. 21. (4) Notwithstanding anything in section 331 of the Criminal Procedure (Scotland) Act 1975, summary proceedings for an offence under this Act may be commenced in Scotland at any time within three years after the commission of the offence and within six months after the date on which evidence sufficient in the opinion of the Lord Advocate to justify the proceedings comes to his knowledge ; and subsection (3) of that section shall apply for the purposes of this subsection as it applies for the purposes of that section.

(5) For the purposes of subsections (3) and (4) above a certificate of the Director of Public Prosecutions or, as the case may be, the Lord Advocate as to the date on which such evidence as is there mentioned came to his knowledge shall be conclusive evidence of that fact.

Repeal, consequential amendments and transitional provisions.

1876 c. 77.
1973 c. 60.

27.—(1) The Cruelty to Animals Act 1876 is hereby repealed.

(2) The enactments mentioned in Schedule 3 to this Act shall have effect with the amendments there specified, being amendments consequential on the provisions of this Act.

(3) The Breeding of Dogs Act 1973 shall not apply to the breeding of dogs for use in regulated procedures if they are bred at a designated breeding establishment.

(4) Schedule 4 to this Act shall have effect with respect to the transitional matters there mentioned.

(5) The Secretary of State may by order make such further transitional provisions as he considers necessary or expedient.

Orders.

28.—(1) Any power of the Secretary of State to make an order under this Act shall be exercisable by statutory instrument.

(2) A statutory instrument containing an order under any of the foregoing provisions of this Act shall be subject to annulment in pursuance of a resolution of either House of Parliament.

Application to Northern Ireland.

29.—(1) This Act applies to Northern Ireland with the following modifications.

(2) For any reference to the Secretary of State in any provision of this Act except sections 19 and 20(1) there shall be

substituted a reference to the Department of Health and Social Services for Northern Ireland; and for the reference in section 18(1) above to the Treasury there shall be substituted a reference to the Department of Finance and Personnel for Northern Ireland.

(3) The functions of the Secretary of State under sections 19 and 20(1) shall be exercisable by him jointly with the Department of Health and Social Services for Northern Ireland; and any notice under section 19(6) or advice under section 20(1) may be given to either of them.

(4) In section 20(5) above for the reference to Parliament there shall be substituted a reference to the Northern Ireland Assembly; and in section 21 above—

    (a) for the references to Parliament or either House of Parliament there shall be substituted references to the Assembly;

    (b) in subsection (5) after the word " if " there shall be inserted the words " within the statutory period (within the meaning of the Interpretation Act (Northern Ireland) 1954) "; and

    (c) subsection (6) shall be omitted.

(5) In sections 22(5) and 26(1)(b) above for the references to section 1 of the Protection of Animals Act 1911 there shall be substituted references to sections 13 and 14 of the Welfare of Animals Act (Northern Ireland) 1972.   1972 c. 7. (N.I.).

(6) In section 25(1) above for the reference to information on oath there shall be substituted a reference to a complaint on oath.

(7) In section 26 above—

    (a) in subsections (1) and (3) for the words " England and Wales " there shall be substituted the words " Northern Ireland ";

    (b) in subsections (1), (3) and (5) for the references to the Director of Public Prosecutions there shall be substituted references to the Director of Public Prosecutions for Northern Ireland; and

    (c) in subsection (3) for the reference to section 127(1) of the Magistrates' Courts Act 1980 there shall be substituted a reference to Article 19(1) of the Magistrates' Courts (Northern Ireland) Order 1981.   S.I. 1981/1675 (N.I.26).

(8) In section 27(3) above for the reference to the Breeding of Dogs Act 1973 there shall be substituted a reference to Articles 12, 13 and 43 of the Dogs (Northern Ireland) Order 1983.   S.I. 1983/1764 (N.I.8).

(9) Section 28 above shall not apply and any order made by the Department of Health and Social Services for Northern Ireland under this Act shall be a statutory rule for the purposes of the Statutory Rules (Northern Ireland) Order 1979 and shall be subject to negative resolution within the meaning of section 41(6) of the Interpretation Act (Northern Ireland) 1954.

S.I. 1979/1573 (N.I.12).

1954 c. 33 (N.I.).

Short title, interpretation and commencement.

30.—(1) This Act may be cited as the Animals (Scientific Procedures) Act 1986.

(2) In this Act—

" designated ", in relation to an establishment, means designated by a certificate under section 6 or 7 above ;

" personal licence " means a licence granted under section 4 above ;

" place " includes any place within the seaward limits of the territorial waters of the United Kingdom, including any vessel other than a ship which is not a British ship ;

" project licence " means a licence granted under section 5 above ;

" protected animal " has the meaning given in section 1 above but subject to any order under subsection (3) of that section ;

" regulated procedure " has the meaning given in section 2 above.

(3) This Act shall come into force on such date as the Secretary of State may by order appoint ; and different dates may be appointed for different provisions or different purposes.

SCHEDULES

SCHEDULE 1

STANDARD METHODS OF HUMANE KILLING

Method	*Animals for which appropriate*
A. *Animals other than foetal, larval and embryonic forms*	
1. Overdose of anaesthetic suitable for the species—	
(i) by injection	(i) All animals.
(ii) by inhalation	(ii) All animals up to 1 kg bodyweight except reptiles, diving birds and diving mammals.
(iii) by immersion.	(iii) Fishes Amphibia up to 250 g bodyweight.
(Followed by destruction of the brain in cold-blooded vertebrates and by exsanguination or by dislocation of the neck in warm blooded vertebrates except where *rigor mortis* has been confirmed).	
2. Dislocation of the neck.	Rodents up to 500g bodyweight other than guinea-pigs.
(Followed by destruction of the brain in fishes).	Guinea-pigs and lagomorphs up to 1 kg bodyweight. Birds up to 3 kg bodyweight. Fishes up to 250g bodyweight.
3. Concussion by striking the back of the head.	Rodents up to 1 kg bodyweight. Birds up to 250 g bodyweight. Fishes.
(Followed by exsanguination or dislocation of the neck in rodents and birds and destruction of the brain in fishes).	
4. Decapitation followed by destruction of the brain.	Cold-blooded vertebrates.
5. Exposure to carbon dioxide in a rising concentration using a suitable technique followed by exsanguination or by dislocation of the neck except where *rigor mortis* has been confirmed.	Rodents over 10 days of age up to 1½ kg bodyweight. Birds over 1 week of age up to 3 kg bodyweight.

B. *Foetal, larval and embryonic forms*

1. Overdose of anaesthetic suitable for the species—

(i) by injection   (i) All animals.

(ii) by immersion.   (ii) Fishes
                          Amphibia.

2. Decapitation.   Mammals.

SCHEDULE 2

ANIMALS TO BE OBTAINED ONLY FROM DESIGNATED BREEDING OR SUPPLYING ESTABLISHMENTS

Mouse
Rat
Guinea-pig
Hamster
Rabbit
Dog
Cat
Primate

SCHEDULE 3

CONSEQUENTIAL AMENDMENTS

1. In section 1(3) of the Protection of Animals Act 1911 for the words " the Cruelty to Animals Act 1876 " there shall be substituted the words " the Animals (Scientific Procedures) Act 1986 ".

2. In section 1(3) of the Protection of Animals (Scotland) Act 1912 for the words " the Cruelty to Animals Act 1876 " there shall be substituted the words " the Animals (Scientific Procedures) Act 1986 ".

3. In paragraph 1 of Schedule 1 to the Protection of Animals (Anaesthetics) Act 1954 for the words " Any experiment duly authorised under the Cruelty to Animals Act 1876 " there shall be substituted the words " Any procedure duly authorised under the Animals (Scientific Procedures) Act 1986 ".

4. In section 12 of the Pests Act 1954 for the words " any experiment duly authorised under the Cruelty to Animals Act 1876 " there shall be substituted the words " any procedure duly authorised under the Animals (Scientific Procedures) Act 1986 ".

5. In section 19(4)(*a*) of the Veterinary Surgeons Act 1966 for the words " any experiment duly authorised under the Cruelty to Animals Act 1876 " there shall be substituted the words " any procedure duly authorised under the Animals (Scientific Procedures) Act 1986 ".

6. In section 1(2A)(*b*) of the Slaughter of Poultry Act 1967 for the words " an experiment in respect of which restrictions are imposed by the Cruelty to Animals Act 1876, being an experiment performed subject to any restrictions so imposed " there shall be substituted the words " a procedure duly authorised under the Animals (Scientific Procedures) Act 1986 ". SCH. 3
1967 c. 24.

7. In section 1(2) of the Agriculture (Miscellaneous Provisions) Act 1968 for the words " the Cruelty to Animals Act 1876 " there shall be substituted the words " the Animals (Scientific Procedures) Act 1986 ". 1968 c. 34.

8. In sections 1(2) and 15(*a*) of, and paragraph 1 of Schedule 1 to, the Welfare of Animals Act (Northern Ireland) 1972 for the words " the Cruelty to Animals Act 1876 " there shall be substituted the words " the Animals (Scientific Procedures) Act 1986 ". 1972 c. 7 (N.I.).

9. In section 8(3) of the Badgers Act 1973 for the words from " something done " onwards there shall be substituted the words " doing anything which is authorised under the Animals (Scientific Procedures) Act 1986 ". 1973 c. 57.

10. In section 5(4) of the Dangerous Wild Animals Act 1976 for the words " registered pursuant to the Cruelty to Animals Act 1876 for the purpose of performing experiments " there shall be substituted the words " which is a designated establishment within the meaning of the Animals (Scientific Procedures) Act 1986 ". 1976 c. 38.

SCHEDULE 4

Section 27 (4).

TRANSITIONAL PROVISIONS

(not reproduced here)

Appendix II:

STANDARD CONDITIONS: DESIGNATED SCIENTIFIC PROCEDURE ESTABLISHMENTS

1. The establishment shall be maintained substantially as at the time the certificate of designation was granted, except where variations are authorised by the Secretary of State.

2. Unless authorised by the Secretary of State, there shall be no variation of the use of the approved rooms and other places in the designated establishment which may have consequences for the protected animals held.

3. Unless otherwise authorised by the Secretary of State, only the types of protected animals specified in the certificate may be accommodated in the establishment.

4. The establishment shall be appropriately staffed at all times to ensure the well-being of the protected animals.

5. Unless otherwise authorised in a project licence, none of the following animals shall be allowed to be used in a procedure unless it has been bred at a designated breeding establishment or obtained from a designated supplying establishment: *mouse, rat, guinea-pig, hamster, rabbit, primate*. Furthermore, unless otherwise authorised in a project licence, no *cat or dog* shall be used unless it has been bred at and obtained from a designated establishment.

6. The certificate holder shall ensure that records are maintained of the source, use and final disposal of all protected animals accommodated in the establishment for scientific purposes and that such records are available to be seen by the Inspector or for submission to the Secretary of State.

7. A health record relating to all protected animals kept for scientific purposes and accommodated in the establishment shall be maintained under the supervision of the named veterinary surgeon and be readily available for examination by the Inspector.

8. All primates, cats and dogs which are used or intended for use in procedures shall be clearly and adequately identifiable by a method of marking agreed with the Inspector.

9. In accordance with the *Code of Practice for the Housing and Care of Animals used in Scientific Procedures,* all protected animals must at all times be provided with adequate care and accommodation appropriate to their type or species; and environmental conditions in all parts of the establishment where protected animals are kept shall be checked at least once daily.

10. The person(s) named in the certificate as responsible for the day-to-day care of animals shall ensure that any protected animal which is not the immediate responsibility of any personal licensee and is found to be in severe pain or severe distress which cannot be alleviated shall be painlessly killed at once in accordance with condition 17 below.

11. In any case where it appears to the named veterinary surgeon(s) or to the named person(s) responsible for the day-to-day care of the animals that the health or the welfare of a protected animal kept for experimental or other scientific

purposes at the establishment gives rise to concern, he shall notify the personal licensee who is in charge of the animal. If there is no such licensee, or if he is not available, the named veterinary surgeon or the named person responsible for the day-to-day care of the animal shall take steps to ensure that the animal is cared for or, if necessary, painlessly killed in accordance with condition 17 below.

12.   Arrangements to ensure that animals are given adequate care must be made in the event that the named persons are not available for any reason such as leave or sickness.

13.   Adequate security measures shall be maintained to prevent the escape of protected animals and to prevent intrusions by unauthorised persons.

14.   Quarantine and acclimatisation facilities shall be provided as necessary.

15.   Adequate precautions against fire shall be maintained at all times.

16.   The certificate holder shall take all reasonable steps to prevent the performance of unauthorised procedures in the establishment.

17.   In any case where it is intended to kill a protected animal which has been kept at the establishment for scientific purposes but is not required to be killed under the terms of the project licence, the method of killing employed must be one which is appropriate under Schedule 1 to the Act or a method authorised in the special conditions of this certificate. The certificate holder shall ensure that a person competent to kill animals in accordance with these conditions is available.

18.   Inspectors shall be provided with access at all reasonable times to all parts of the establishment which are concerned with the use, holding or care of protected animals.

19.   The certificate holder shall take steps to provide such training as is necessary for all licensees carrying out regulated procedures.

20.   The certificate holder shall notify the Secretary of State of any proposed change in:

  (i)   the title of the designated establishment;

  (ii)   the full name of the certificate holder;

  (iii)   the full name(s) and qualifications of the person(s) responsible for the day-to-day care of the protected animals;

  (iv)   the full name(s) of the veterinary surgeon(s).

21.   The certificate holder shall notify the Secretary of State of the death of a project licence holder within seven days of its coming to his knowledge when, unless the Secretary of State directs otherwise, the project licence shall continue in force for 28 days from the date of notification.

22.   A copy of these conditions shall be readily available for consultation by all licensees and named persons in the establishment.

Appendix III:

STANDARD CONDITIONS: DESIGNATED BREEDING AND
SUPPLYING ESTABLISHMENTS

1. In these conditions the word "animals" means any of the species listed in Schedule 2 to the Act: *mouse, rat, guinea-pig, hamster, rabbit, dog, cat and primate*.

2. The establishment shall be maintained substantially as at the time the certificate of designation was granted, except where variations are authorised by the Secretary of State.

3. Unless authorised by the Secretary of State, there shall be no variation of the use of the approved rooms and other places in the designated establishment which may have consequences for the protected animals held.

4. The establishment shall be appropriately staffed at all times to ensure the well-being of the animals.

5. The certificate holder shall ensure that records are maintained of the source, use and final disposal of all protected animals bred, kept for breeding or kept for subsequent supply for use for scientific purposes and that such records are available to be seen by the Inspector or for submission to the Secretary of State.

6. A health record relating to all protected animals bred, kept for breeding, or kept for subsequent supply for use for scientific purposes and accommodated in the establishment, shall be maintained under the supervision of the named veterinary surgeon and be readily available for examination by the Inspector.

7. All primates, cats and dogs accommodated in the establishment which are bred or intended for breeding or supplying for use for scientific purposes shall be clearly and adequately identifiable by an acceptable method of marking agreed with the Inspector.

8. Unless otherwise authorised by the Secretary of State, animals must be obtained from designated breeding or supplying establishments.

9. All animals must at all times be provided with adequate care and accommodation appropriate to their type or species; and environmental conditions in all parts of the establishment where these animals are kept shall be checked at least once daily.

10. The person named in the certificate as responsible for the day-to-day care of animals shall ensure that any animal which is found to be in severe pain or severe distress which cannot be alleviated shall be painlessly killed at once in accordance with condition 16 below.

11. In any case where it appears to the named veterinary surgeon or to the named person responsible for the day-to-day care of the animals that the health or the welfare of an animal at the establishment gives rise to concern he or she shall take steps to ensure that the animal is either cared for or, if necessary, painlessly killed.

12. Arrangements to ensure that animals are given adequate care must be made in the event that the named persons referred to in condition 18(iii) below are not available for any reason such as leave or sickness.

13.   Adequate security measures shall be maintained to prevent the escape of protected animals and to prevent intrusions by unauthorised persons.

14.   Quarantine and acclimatisation facilities shall be provided as necessary.

15.   Adequate precautions against fire shall be maintained at all times.

16.   In any case where it is intended to kill a protected animal which has been bred, kept for breeding or kept for subsequent supply for use for scientific purposes then the method of killing employed must be one which is appropriate under Schedule 1 to the Act or a method authorised in the special conditions of this certificate. The certificate holder shall ensure that a person competent to kill animals in accordance with these conditions is available.

17   Inspectors shall be provided with access at all reasonable times to all parts of the establishment relating to the holding or care of protected animals.

18.   The certificate holder shall notify the Secretary of State of any proposed change in:

(i)   the title of the designated establishment;

(ii)   the full name of the certificate holder;

(iii)   the full name(s) and qualifications of the person(s) responsible for the day-to-day care of the protected animals;

(iv)   the full name(s) of the veterinary surgeon(s).

19.   A copy of these conditions shall be readily available for consultation by all persons in the establishment responsible for the health, care and welfare of animals.

Appendix IV:

STANDARD CONDITIONS: PROJECT LICENCES

The authority conferred by this licence is subject to the following conditions. Licences may be revoked or varied for a breach of conditions.

In addition, breaches of conditions 1 to 5 may be criminal offences under the Act.

1. No person shall carry out any procedure authorised by the project licence unless also authorised to do so by a personal licence.

2. Procedures under the authority of the project licence shall be carried out only at the place or places specified in the licence, unless their performance elsewhere is authorised by the Secretary of State.

3. No person working under the authority of the project licence shall use any neuromuscular blocking agent in place of an anaesthetic.

4. No person working under the authority of the project licence shall use any neuromuscular blocking agent without express authority from the Secretary of State which must be contained in both the project and personal licences.

5. No animal may be used again on the same protocol, or on another protocol, whether on the same licence or another, without express authority in this project licence.

6. In any procedure, the degree of severity imposed shall be the minimum consistent with the attainment of the objects of the procedure.

7. Except with the authorisation of the Secretary of State, none of the following animals shall be used in any regulated procedure unless it has been bred at a breeding establishment or obtained from a supplying establishment designated by a certificate issued under the Act: *mouse, rat, guinea-pig, hamster, rabbit and primate*. Furthermore, except with the authorisation of the Secretary of State, no *cat or dog* shall be used under the licence unless it has been bred at and obtained from a designated breeding establishment.

8. It is the responsibility of the project licence holder to ensure as far as possible adherence to the severity limit of each procedure as shown in the listing of protocols (section 19a) and observance of any other controls described for that procedure in the protocol sheet (section 19b). If these constraints appear to have been, or likely to be, exceeded, the project licence holder or a deputy shall notify the Inspector as soon as possible.

9. It is the responsibility of the project licence holder to maintain a record, in a form agreed with the Inspector, of all animals on which procedures have been carried out under the authority of the project licence, showing the procedures used and the names of personal licensees who have carried out the procedures. The record shall be open to examination by the Inspector at any time.

10. The project licence holder shall send to the Secretary of State, before 31 January each year, a report in a form approved by the Secretary of State, giving details of the number of procedures and animals used and the nature of the procedures performed under the authority of the project licence during the year.

11.   The project licence holder shall submit to the Secretary of State titles and references of publications relating to work carried out under authority of this licence as they become available; and shall supply a copy of any such publication if requested to do so.

12.   The project licence holder shall submit such other reports as the Secretary of State may from time to time require.

13.   The project licence holder shall ensure that details of procedures authorised in sections 18 and 19 of the Schedule to this licence and any additional conditions imposed on those procedures are known to all personal licensees performing those procedures.

14.   The project licence holder shall ensure that the appropriate level of supervision is provided for all personal licensees working on the project who are subject to a supervision condition.

15.   The project licence holder must obtain the permission of the Inspector before:

  (i)   any animal undergoing regulated procedures is moved from one designated establishment to another; or

  (ii)   any animal is released for slaughter; or

  (iii)   any animal is released from the controls of the Act;

unless this is already authorised by the project licence.

Appendix V:

RECORD KEEPING IN DESIGNATED SCIENTIFIC PROCEDURE ESTABLISHMENTS, AND BY PROJECT AND PERSONAL LICENCE HOLDERS

1. General

1.1. Licence and certificate conditions which are imposed under the Animals (Scientific Procedures) Act 1986 require the maintenance of records by project licence holders and at all designated scientific procedure establishments. The standard certificate and licence conditions are set out in Appendices II, IV and VI.

1.2. Holders of certificates of designation should ensure that all the records kept for the purposes of the Act are properly maintained and preserved for a period of five years following the death of the animal or its release from the establishment. Records must be kept for each protected animal either individually or in batches (see paragraph 1.4 below).

1.3. For regulated procedures involving fetal, larval or embryonic forms, different records are required depending on the use to which the immature forms are put. Unless otherwise agreed with the Inspector, if the immature forms are for use in regulated procedures which require survival beyond the fetal, larval or embryonic stage of development, individual records will be required; if not, it will normally be necessary to record only batches of such protected animals.

1.4. Adult fish, amphibians, reptiles, unweaned rodents and lagomorphs and non-adult birds may, with the agreement of the Inspector, be recorded in batches until they are used for regulated procedures.

1.5. The requirements set out below are not exhaustive. Additional requirements may be imposed in certain circumstances.

2. Designated scientific procedure establishments

2.1. In the case of dogs, cats, equidae, primates, cattle and other farm animals and adult birds, each animal accommodated in the establishment must be readily identifiable. In the case of dogs, cats and primates this must be by a method of permanent marking agreed with the Inspector.

2.2. Each cage or confinement area holding protected animals not undergoing a regulated procedure should bear a label on which at least the following information is recorded:

    (i)   cage/area identification;

    (ii) identification of animals held (by individual or batch numbers as appropriate);

    (iii) date entry made.

2.3. The following information is to be recorded for all normal animals, pretreated animals or animals with harmful genetic defects:

    (i)   source (and name of breeder or supplier, if animal was bred elsewhere);

(ii)   species;

(iii) breed or strain;

(iv)   identification (by individual or batch number as appropriate);

(v)   date of arrival (or, if the animal was bred at the establishment, the date of transfer to holding unit or user unit);

(vi)   approximate age on arrival;

(vii) sex;

(viii) if female, whether pregnant or not;

(ix)   dates in and out of quarantine or isolation, if appropriate;

(x)   microbiological status (gnotobiotic, SPF or conventional);

(xi)   pretreatment, if any;

(xii) harmful genetic defects, if any;

(xiii) project licence to which allocated or other disposal.

2.4.   A health record relating to the protected animals kept at the designated establishment must be maintained under the supervision of the veterinary surgeon or other suitably qualified person named in the certificate of designation. It will be for the named veterinary surgeon, (or other suitably qualified person, where appointed) to decide upon the form of the health record, in consultation with the certificate holder, licensees and the Inspector.

3.   Records to be maintained under the control of project licence holders

3.1.   Condition 9 of the standard licence conditions for project licences requires the holder to maintain a record, in a form agreed with the Inspector, of all animals on which procedures have been carried out under the authority of the project licence, showing the procedures used and the names of personal licensees who have carried out the procedures on the animals. The record has to be open to examination by the Inspector at any time.

3.2.   The record should include the following information:

(i)   name of the project licence holder, deputy project licence holder (where applicable) and project licence number;

(ii)   name(s) of personal licensees involved;

(iii) details of procedures to include:
   (a)   species of protected animals used;
   (b)   number of each species used (running tally);
   (c)   sex and approximate age at commencement of the regulated procedure;
   (d)   identification of protected animal (where appropriate);
   (e)   date of commencement of the regulated procedure;
   (f)   any unexpected morbidity or mortality;
   (g)   brief description of procedures used;
   (h)   re-use within the project (for re-use after general anaesthesia include certificate of fitness for re-use obtained from veterinary surgeon or other suitably qualified person if appointed);
   (j)   date of end of the regulated procedures;

(iv)   fate of animals at the end of the regulated procedures, ie whether released to the wild; dispatched to private care; released for slaughter; killed within the establishment; or if permission for re-use was granted, identification of the project to which the animal was allocated.

4. Records to be maintained by personal licensee

4.1. It is the responsibility of the personal licensees to ensure that all cages or enclosures are clearly labelled.

4.2. The labelling must be such as to enable the Inspector to identify the project on which the animals are being used, the responsible personal licensee and the principal procedures involved.

4.3. Labelling can be carried out by the use of codes, so that none of the information can be obtained directly from the cage label, provided that there are effective arrangements for the information to be decoded for the Inspector.

4.4. Personal licensees should ensure that records are kept of all procedures performed and whether they were supervised.

Appendix VI:

STANDARD CONDITIONS: PERSONAL LICENCES

The authority conferred by this licence is subject to the following conditions. Licences may be revoked or varied for a breach of conditions.

In addition, breaches of conditions 1-9 and failure to comply with a requirement under condition 10 may be criminal offences under the Act.

1.   No personal licensee shall carry out a regulated procedure for which authority has not been granted in his or her personal licence.

2.   No personal licensee shall use in any regulated procedure any type of protected animal not authorised by his or her personal licence.

3.   No personal licensee shall carry out any regulated procedure unless authorised by a project licence.

4.   No personal licensee shall carry out any regulated procedure as an exhibition to the general public or carry out any such procedure which is shown live on television for general reception.

5.   No personal licensee carrying out any regulated procedure shall use any neuromuscular blocking agent in place of an anaesthetic.

6.   No personal licensee shall use any neuromuscular blocking agent without express authority from the Secretary of State which must be contained in both the project and personal licences.

7.   Personal licensees shall perform the procedures for which they have authority only at the place or places specified in their personal licences, unless their performance elsewhere is authorised by the Secretary of State in both project and personal licences.

8.   Any animal which at the conclusion of a series of procedures for a particular purpose is suffering or is likely to suffer adverse effects shall forthwith be humanely killed by a method appropriate to the animal under Schedule 1 to the Act, or by a method authorised by the personal licence of the person by whom the animal is killed.

9.   No animal may be re-used without express authority in the project licence.

10.   If an Inspector requires that an animal must be killed because it is undergoing excessive suffering, it must be immediately and painlessly killed by a method appropriate to the animal under Schedule 1 to the Act, or by a method authorised by the personal licence of the person by whom the animal is killed.

11.   It is the responsibility of a personal licensee to ensure that all cages, pens or other enclosures are clearly labelled. The labelling must be such as to enable the Inspector and named persons to identify the project in which the animals are being used, the responsible personal licensee and the principal procedures involved.

12.   The personal licensee must take effective precautions, including the use of sedatives, tranquillisers, analgesics or anaesthetics, to prevent or reduce to the minimum level consistent with the aims of the procedure any pain, suffering, distress or discomfort in the animals used.

13.   It is the responsibility of the personal licensee to notify the project licence holder as soon as possible when it appears either that the severity limit of any procedure listed in the project licence (section 19a) or that the constraints upon adverse effects described in the protocol sheets (seciton 19b) have been or are likely to be significantly exceeded.

14.   In all circumstances where an animal which is being or has been subjected to a regulated procedure is in severe pain or severe distress which cannot be alleviated the personal licensee must ensure that the animal is painlessly killed forthwith by a method appropriate to the animal under Schedule 1 to the Act or by such other method as may be authorised by the licence.

15.   It is the responsibility of the personal licensee to ensure that suitable arrangements exist for the care and welfare of animals during any period when the licensee is not in attendance.

16.   It is the responsibility of the personal licensee to ensure that, whenever necessary, veterinary advice and treatment are obtained for the animals in his or her care.

17.   Where a personal licence is issued subject to a condition of supervision the personal licensee must adhere to the requirements of the supervisor.

18.   Before any animal or group of animals that has been subject to procedures is released into the wild, to a farm, or for use as a pet, the personal licensee must ensure that authority exists in the project licence for the animal to be released.

19.   When anaesthesia (whether general, regional or local) is used, it shall be of sufficient depth to prevent the animal from being aware of pain arising during the procedure.

Appendix VII:

EXAMPLES OF THE KINDS OF PROCEDURES WHICH MAY, WITH PERMISSION, BE DELEGATED TO NON-LICENSED ASSISTANTS

In certain circumstances, it may be possible for personal licensees to delegate the conduct of certain regulated procedures to non-licensees. As it is not easy to provide an exhaustive list of the kind of tasks which may be delegated, this appendix contains some examples. In all cases, specific authority to delegate must be contained in the personal licence.

Non-technical procedures

Wherever the list below refers to tasks "previously" carried out, those tasks will have been specified by a suitably qualified personal licensee, *who must be within reach for assistance or advice if required*.

1.   The filling of food hoppers and water bottles with previously mixed diets or liquids of altered constitution or to which test substances have been previously added.

2.   The placing of animals in some previously set-up altered environments, eg inhalation chambers, pressure chambers, aquatic environments.

3.   Pressing the exposure button to deliver previously determined doses of irradiation to an animal.

4.   Pairing/grouping associated with the breeding of animals with harmful genetic defects.

5.   Withdrawal of contents from an established ruminal fistula.

6.   Operating automated machinery which carries out inoculation of eggs.

7.   Placement of animals in restraining devices, as defined by the project licence.

8.   Withdrawal of food and/or water, as defined by the project licence.

9.   Placement of avian eggs into previously-set chillers at the termination of a procedure.

Tasks which may be undertaken by assistants only in the presence of a suitably authorised personal licensee

10.   In animals rendered insentient by decerebration or general anaesthesia which is to persist until death, and through an established catheter, administration of a substance(s) as defined by the project licence or removal of body fluids.

11.   In animals rendered insentient by decerebration or general anaesthesia which is to persist until death, the administration of electric stimuli through electrodes implanted by a personal licensee.

Appendix VIII:

PROCEDURE FOR REPRESENTATIONS UNDER THE ANIMALS (SCIENTIFIC PROCEDURES) ACT 1986

Explanatory note issued to applicants who may wish to make representations

Introduction

1.   This note describes the procedure to be followed if you intend to exercise your right under the Animals (Scientific Procedures) Act 1986 to make written and, if you wish, oral representations against the Secretary of State's proposal to revoke, or vary, or not to vary the conditions of any licence or certificate issued to you under the Act, or to refuse your application for a licence or certificate under the Act.

2.   Section 12 of the Act provides that if you make representations, a legally qualified person (who must be a person who holds, or has held, judicial office in the United Kingdom, or a barrister, solicitor or advocate of at least seven years' standing) will be appointed to consider them and report to the Secretary of State. The Secretary of State will take the report into account when making a final decision upon your licence, certificate or application.

Notification

3.   You should notify the Secretary of State of your wish to make representations and say whether you wish to make oral or written representations or both, by the date shown in the notice. This will not be less than 28 days from the date of service of the notice. Once your notification has been received, the Secretary of State will inform you of the name of the legally qualified person appointed to consider the matter and the address to which you may send any written representations.

Documents

4.   At the same time, the Secretary of State will send to you and to the person appointed to consider your representations, a copy of the list of documents he considers relevant to the consideration of your case, together with a copy of each document.

Time limit for written representations

5.   You should submit your written representations to the person appointed to consider your case within 21 days of the date you are notified of his appointment and sent the relevant documents. This period may be extended at the discretion of the person appointed.

Notice of hearing of oral representations

6.   If you have asked to make oral representations, you will be given at least 28 days' notice in writing of the date, time and place of the hearing. At the same

time you will be asked to state whether you wish the hearing to be in public. In addition, if you wish to dispute any fact contained in a report from the Inspector, you should give notice of this to the Secretary of State and provided you give at least seven days' notice, the Inspector will attend the hearing and you will be entitled to question him about any matter of fact contained in the report.

Procedure at hearings of oral representations

7. The person appointed to hear your representations will determine the procedure to be followed at the hearing. You may attend the hearing if you wish. You may also be represented at the hearing by another person who may or may not be a lawyer. You have a right to call witnesses and to address the person appointed. The hearing will only be held in public if you have asked for this, but any hearing may be attended by a member of the Council on Tribunals or of its Scottish Committee.

Decision

8. The person appointed will provide a written report and recommendation to the Secretary of State. The Secretary of State will send you a copy with his final decision.

Appendix IX:

S T A T U T O R Y   I N S T R U M E N T S

1986 No. 1911

ANIMALS

The Animals (Scientific Procedures) (Procedure for Representations) Rules 1986

Made - - - - -	*7th November* 1986
Laid before Parliament	*18th November* 1986
Coming into Operation	*10th December* 1986

In exercise of the powers conferred on me by section 12(7) of the Animals (Scientific Procedures) Act 1986(**a**), I hereby make the following Rules:—

Citation, commencement and extent

1. These Rules may be cited as the Animals (Scientific Procedures) (Procedure for Representations) Rules 1986 and shall come into operation on 10th December 1986.

2. These Rules shall apply to England and Wales and Scotland.

Interpretation, etc.

3.—(1) In these Rules—

"the Act" means the Animals (Scientific Procedures) Act 1986;

"applicant" means an applicant for a licence or certificate under the Act or the holder of such a licence or certificate who wishes to make written or oral representations in respect of a proposal to refuse, vary or revoke such a licence or certificate or the inclusion of any condition in such a licence or certificate under section 12(3) or (4) of the Act; and

"person appointed" means a person appointed to receive such representations under section 12 of the Act.

(2) Any notification, notice, written representations or other document given or sent in pursuance of these Rules may be given or sent by post.

Notification of appointment

4. Where the applicant has notified the Secretary of State of his wish to make representations under section 12(3) or (4) of the Act, the Secretary of State shall notify the applicant in writing of the name of the person appointed and of the address to which his written representations are to be sent.

(**a**) 1986 c. 14.

Documents
5. The Secretary of State shall prepare a list of the documents which he considers relevant to the consideration of representations by the person appointed and shall send a copy of such list, together with a copy of each of the documents included in it, to the applicant with the notification sent in pursuance of the preceding Rule, and to the person appointed.

Time limit for written representations
6. The applicant shall submit his written representations under section 12(3) or (4) to the person appointed not later than 21 days after the date on which he is notified of the appointment of the person appointed in pursuance of Rule 4 of these Rules; but the person appointed may, if he thinks fit, extend the period during which such representations are to be submitted to him.

Notice of hearing of oral representations
7.—(1) Where the applicant has notified the Secretary of State of his wish to make oral representations under section 12(3) or (4) of the Act, the Secretary of State shall give him at least 28 days' notice in writing of the date, time and place of the hearing by the person appointed.

(2) Such notice shall request the applicant to state whether he wishes the hearing to be in public.

(3) Such notice shall, where the documents sent in pursuance of Rule 5 of these Rules include a report by an inspector appointed under section 18 of the Act, invite the applicant to notify the Secretary of State whether he intends to dispute any fact contained in that report; and where the applicant has given the Secretary of State at least 7 days' notice of his intention to dispute any such fact, the inspector shall attend the hearing and the applicant shall be entitled to question him about any matter of fact contained in the report.

Procedure at hearings of oral representations
8.—(1) Subject to the provisions of the Act and the other provisions of these Rules the person appointed shall, in his discretion, determine the procedure at the hearing of oral representations.

(2) The applicant may appear in person at such a hearing, or may be represented by any other person, and shall be entitled to call witnesses and to address the person appointed.

(3) If the applicant so requests, the hearing by the person appointed shall be in public.

(4) Any member of the Council on Tribunals or of the Scottish Committee of the Council in his capacity as such may attend any hearing by a person appointed.

Postponement or adjournment
9. The person appointed may, if he thinks fit, postpone or adjourn any hearing of oral representations pending before him, and shall give the applicant reasonable notice of the date, time and place of the subsequent hearing.

Appointed person's report

10. Following his consideration of representations, the person appointed shall prepare a written report of his findings and recommendation and send it to the Secretary of State who shall furnish a copy of it to the applicant.

Home Office.
7th November 1986.

Douglas Hurd,
One of Her Majesty's Principal
Secretaries of State.

EXPLANATORY NOTE

(This Note is not part of the Rules.)

Section 12 of the Animals (Scientific Procedures) Act 1986 confers a right to make representations to a legally qualified person appointed by the Secretary of State on a person who has applied for or holds a personal or project licence or a certificate of designation of a scientific procedure, breeding or supplying establishment under that Act where the Secretary of State proposes to refuse such a licence or certificate or to vary or revoke it otherwise than at the request of the holder, or where the holder is dissatisfied with any condition contained in such a licence or certificate. These Rules prescribe the procedure to be followed in the making and consideration of such representations.

Printed in the United Kingdom for HMSO

Dd 0504654   2/90   C30   60305   3383/2   91671   2019

HMSO also publishes:

Code of Practice for the Housing and Care of Animals Used in Scientific Procedures (1989; HC 107; price £4.90p)

and, each year,

Report of the Animals Procedures Committee (1988; HC 458; price £3.20p)

Statistics of Scientific Procedures on Living Animals, Great Britain (1988; Cm 743; price £7.50p)

ORDER FORM

	Numbers	Cost
Guidance on the Operation of the Animals (Scientific Procedures) Act 1986 (1990: HC 182; price £7.20). Code of Practice for the Housing and Care of Animals used in Scientific Procedures (1989; HC 107; price £4.90.)		
ANNUAL PUBLICATIONS: Report of the Animals Procedures Committee (Price £3.20) Statistics of Scientific Procedures on Living Animals, Great Britain. (Price £7.50)		
TOTAL		£

To obtain the above please send a photocopy of this form to the addresses shown below or telephone the numbers given.

HMSO publications are available from:

HMSO Publications Centre
(Mail and telephone orders only)
PO Box 276, London SW8 5DT
Telephone orders 01-873 9090
General enquiries 01-873 0011
(queuing system in operation for both numbers)

HMSO Bookshops
49 High Holborn, London, WC1V 6HB 01-873 0011 (Counter service only)
258 Broad Street, Birmingham, B1 2HE 021-643 3740
Southey House, 33 Wine Street, Bristol, BS1 2BQ (0272) 264306
9-21 Princess Street, Manchester, M60 8AS 061-834 7201
80 Chichester Street, Belfast, BT1 4JY (0232) 238451
71 Lothian Road, Edinburgh, EH3 9AZ 031-228 4181

HMSO's Accredited Agents
(see Yellow Pages)

And through good booksellers

From 6 May 1990 the London telephone numbers above carry the prefix
'071' instead of '01'.